Oxford Progressive English Readers
General Editor: D.H. Howe

The Gifts and Other Stories

The *Oxford Progressive English Readers* series provides a
wide range of reading for learners of English. It includes
classics, the favourite stories of young readers, and also
modern fiction. The series has five grades: the *Introductory
Grade* at a 1400 word level, *Grade 1* at a 2100 word level,
Grade 2 at a 3100 word level, *Grade 3* at a 3700 word level
and *Grade 4* which consists of abridged stories. Structural
as well as lexical controls are applied at each level.

Wherever possible the mood and style of the original
stories have been retained. Where this requires departure
from the grading scheme, glosses and notes are given.

All the books in the series are attractively illustrated.
Each book also has a short section containing questions and
suggested activities for students.

The Gifts and Other Stories
O. Henry & Others

Hong Kong
OXFORD UNIVERSITY PRESS
Oxford Singapore Tokyo

Oxford University Press

Oxford London New York Toronto
Kuala Lumpur Singapore Hong Kong Tokyo
Delhi Bombay Calcutta Madras Karachi
Nairobi Dar es Salaam Cape Town
Melbourne Auckland

and associated companies in
Beirut Berlin Ibadan Mexico City Nicosia

© Oxford University Press 1974
First published 1974
Tenth impression 1984

OXFORD is a trade mark of Oxford University Press

Retold by A. Toyne
Illustrated by B. Chau
Simplified according to the language grading scheme
especially compiled by D.H. Howe

ISBN 0 19 580574 7

Printed in Hong Kong by Liang Yu Printing Factory Ltd.
Published by Oxford University Press, Warwick House, Hong Kong

Contents

		Page
1	The Gifts *by O. Henry*	1
2	The Country of the Blind *by H. G. Wells*	6
3	The Two Friends *by Guy de Maupassant*	21
4	The Bear-hunt *by Leo Tolstoy*	28
5	The Paradise of Thieves *by G. K. Chesterton*	38
6	'Blow Up with the Ship!' *by Wilkie Collins*	51
7	The Speckled Band *by Sir Arthur Conan Doyle*	61
8	The Goblins and the Grave-digger *by Charles Dickens*	78
9	The Island of Voices *by R. L. Stevenson*	88
10	The Nightingale and the Rose *by Oscar Wilde*	100
	Questions	107

The Gifts

One dollar and eighty-seven cents. That was all she had saved. Three times Della counted it. Only one dollar and eighty-seven cents. And the next day would be Christmas.

There was clearly nothing she could do now but fall down on the old worn couch* and cry. So Della did. You see life is made up of tears and smiles — but mainly of tears.

When Della had finished crying she patted her cheeks with face-powder. She stood by the window and looked out sadly at a grey cat walking along a grey fence in a grey garden. To-morrow would be Christmas Day, and she had only $1.87 with which to buy Jim, her husband, a present. She had been saving every cent she could for months; but twenty dollars a week — which was the total of their income — doesn't leave much for saving. Expenses had been greater than she had calculated. They always are. And now she had only $1.87 to buy a present for Jim. Many happy hours she had spent trying to think of something nice for him. Something fine and rare — something good enough to belong to her Jim.

There was a mirror between the windows of the room. Suddenly she turned away from the window and stood in front of the mirror. Her eyes were shining brightly, but her face had lost its colour within twenty seconds. Rapidly she pulled down her hair and let it fall to its full length.

Now, Della and Jim had two possessions they were very proud of. One was Jim's gold watch, which had been his father's and his grandfather's. The other was Della's lovely, brown, shining hair. It reached to below her knees; and when she let it hang freely, it fell around her like a beautiful cloak*.

Nervously and quickly she pinned up her hair again. She

*couch, a long bed-like seat for sitting or lying on during the day.
*cloak, a piece of clothing, usually without sleeves, worn loosely over
    clothes instead of a coat.

hesitated for a minute and stood still while a tear or two splashed onto the worn red carpet.

She put on her old brown jacket and her old brown hat. Then, with her eyes still shining brightly, she ran out of the door and down the stairs to the street. 5

She stopped at a shop where the sign said: 'Madame Sofonia. We Buy Hair Goods of All Kinds.' Della ran up the steps and paused for a moment at the top to get back her breath. She opened the door.

'Will you buy my hair?' asked Della. 10

'Yes, I buy hair,' said Madame. 'Take off your hat and let's have a look at it.'

Down fell that pile of brown hair.

'Twenty dollars,' said Madame, lifting the hair in an expert way. 15

'Give it to me quickly,' said Della.

Della buys the present

The next two hours passed by happily. She was looking in the shops for Jim's present.

She found it at last. It surely had been made for Jim and no one else. There was not another one like it in all the shops, 20 and she had searched them all carefully. It was a gold watch chain, simple in design. Like all good things, it was its simplicity, and not a lot of decoration, which showed its real value. Clearly, it was good enough for The Watch. As soon as she saw it she knew it must be Jim's. It was just right for him. 25 Although Jim's watch was beautiful, he sometimes looked ashamed because of the old leather strap he used instead of a chain. It cost her twenty-one dollars, and she hurried home with it held tightly in her hand.

When Della reached home she was no longer excited, for 30 now she felt a little worried about what she had done. She looked at what remained of her hair, and then started to work at it with her quick fingers.

In less than forty minutes her head was covered with tiny curls, which made her look like a naughty schoolboy. When 35 she had finished she examined carefully her reflection in the mirror.

At 7 o'clock the coffee was made and she had the pots and pans ready on the stove to cook the supper.

5 Jim was never late. Della sat on the edge of the table nearest the door. She had the gold watch chain hidden in her hand. Then she heard him at the bottom of the stairs, and she turned pale just for a moment. She had the habit of saying little silent prayers about the simplest everyday things, and
10 now she whispered: 'Please God, make him think I'm still pretty.'

The door opened and Jim stepped in. He looked thin and very serious. Poor man, he was only twenty-two and responsible for a family! He needed a new coat and his shoes were
15 old and worn.

A shock for Jim

Jim closed the door. Then he stood still. He began to stare at Della, and there was an expression in his eyes which she could not understand. It frightened her. It was not anger, nor surprise, nor horror, nor any of the feelings she had been pre-
20 pared for. He simply stared at her with a peculiar expression on his face.

Della slid off the table and went to him.

'Jim!' she cried, 'don't look at me that way. I had my hair cut off and sold it because I couldn't have lived through
25 Christmas without giving you a present. It'll grow again — you don't mind, do you? I just had to do it. My hair grows very fast, you know. Please say "Merry Christmas!" Jim, and let's be happy. You don't know what a nice — what a beautiful, nice gift I've got for you.'

30 'You've cut your hair?' asked Jim, slowly, as if he had not really understood anything Della had said to him.

'I've cut it off and sold it,' said Della. 'Don't you like me just as well, anyhow? My hair is gone, but I'm just the same!'

Jim looked about the room curiously.

35 'You say your hair is gone?' he said, looking a little stupid.

'You needn't look for it,' said Della. 'It's sold, I tell you —

sold and gone, too. It's Christmas Eve, Jim. Be good to me, because it went for you.'

Jim seemed to wake quickly out of his dream. He took a package from his coat pocket and threw it upon the table.

'Don't make any mistake about me, Della,' he said, 'I don't   5
think there is anything about her hair that could make me like my dear wife any less. But if you unwrap that package you'll see why I was upset for a while at first.'

Her quick white fingers tore at the string and paper. And then an excited scream of joy; and then a very quick female   10
change to tears and cries.

The combs

For there were The Combs — the pair of combs which for months Della had been going to look at in a shop window. Beautiful combs, real tortoise-shell* with jewelled edges. And they were just the colour to wear in her beautiful hair — if   15
she still had it! They were expensive combs, she knew, and she had wanted them so much; but she had never dreamed that they would ever be hers. And now they were hers, but because her hair was gone she would have no use for them.

However, she held them close to her chest, and at last she   20
was able to look up through her tears and smile and say: 'My hair grows so fast, Jim!'

Then Della remembered something else and cried, 'Oh, oh!'

Jim had not yet seen his beautiful gift. Eagerly she held it out to him in her open hand. The precious metal seemed to   25
flash with a reflection of her bright and warm spirit.

'Isn't it lovely, Jim? I searched all over town for it. You'll have to look at the time a hundred times a day now. Give me your watch. I want to see how it looks on it.'

Instead of obeying, Jim dropped down on the old couch,   30
put his hands on his head, and smiled.

'Della,' said he, 'let's put away our Christmas gifts and keep them for a while. They're too nice to use just now. I sold the watch to get money to buy your combs.

— And now, let's have our supper.'   35

*tortoise-shell, a plastic-like material made from the polished shell of the tortoise.

The Country of the Blind

In a lonely part of South America there is a mysterious
mountain valley, separated from the world of men, called the
Country of the Blind. Many years ago it was possible for men
to travel through the dangerous mountains and reach this
5   wonderful place. A few people did indeed go, a family or so
from Peru who were trying to escape from an evil ruler. Then
came a great earthquake,* followed by landslides* and sudden floods. One side of an old mountain slipped and came
down with a noise like thunder; and so the Country of the
10   Blind became separated from the outside world for ever.

The valley had in it everything that anyone could want —
sweet water, grassy meadows*, a good climate, and slopes of
rich brown soil with small trees that bore excellent fruit.
The people did very well there, and their animals soon in-
15   creased in numbers. But one thing spoiled their happiness,
although it did not spoil it greatly. A strange disease spread
among them which made all the children born in the valley
blind.

As they grew up, the blind children were guided round the
20   valley until they knew it perfectly; and when at last the older
people died, the younger ones lived on. In spite of their
blindness, they even learned to control fire, which they made
carefully in stone stoves.

Generation* followed generation. They forgot many things;
25   they invented many things. Except for their sight, they were
strong and healthy. They increased in numbers and in under-
standing, and they solved all the social and economic problems that arose. Generation followed generation. Then came

*earthquake, sudden and violent shaking of the earth's surface.
*landslide, the sliding down of large amounts of earth and rock, etc.
*meadow, an area of grassland.
*generation, all people born about the same time.

a time when a man from the outside world arrived by chance in the valley. And this is the story of that man.

He was a mountaineer. His name was Nunez. He was a member of a group who had been climbing the almost vertical side of one of the highest mountains of the district. They built a shelter one night in the snow on a little shelf of rock. Later they noticed Nunez was missing. They shouted, but there was no reply. They shouted and whistled, and they did not sleep for the rest of the night.

When the morning came they saw the marks of his fall. He had slipped towards the unknown side of the mountain. Far below he had hit a steep slope of snow, then he had fallen down in the middle of a pile of loose snow. Far, far below, in the distance, they could see trees rising out of a narrow valley — the lost Country of the Blind. But they did not know it was the lost Country of the Blind, nor did they notice if it was in any way different from the other deep valleys. They were frightened by the accident, and so they stopped searching in the afternoon and went back down the other side of the mountain to their camp.

At the end of the slope he fell a thousand feet, and came down in a cloud of snow upon a slope even steeper than the one above. Down this he rolled unconscious, but without a bone broken in his body. At last he came to gentler slopes where he stopped rolling and lay still in the deep snow. He lay upon his chest resting for a while, wondering where he was and what had happened to him. He felt his limbs, and then he discovered that several of his buttons had gone and that his coat was turned over his head. His knife was gone from his pocket and his hat was lost, though he had tied it under his chin. He remembered he had been looking for loose stones to build the shelter wall.

Slowly he got to his feet, aching in every limb, and painfully he climbed down the pile of loose snow around him. He went down to where the snow was thinner and finally disappeared, and there he sat leaning against a large rock, and immediately fell asleep.

The land below the cliff

He was awakened by the singing of the birds in the trees far below. He sat up and saw that he was at the foot of a huge cliff. Below him it seemed there was a slope equally steep, but he found a way down through a wide crack in the rock, like a chimney. This looked extremely dangerous, and it was all wet with melting snow. But, he found it easier than it appeared, and at last he came into the valley and the sunlight. He was stiff and weary. He sat down in the shadow of a rock for a while to rest before he went to the houses.

They were strange to his eyes, and indeed the whole appearance of the valley became, as he looked at it, stranger and more unfamiliar. Most of its surface was soft green meadow, covered with beautiful flowers. On the higher slopes flocks of llamas* were eating the sweet grass. Huts, which must have been shelters or eating-places for the llamas, stood against the boundary wall here and there. A number of paths made of black and white stones, and each with an unusual little stone edge, ran in different directions in an orderly manner. The houses of the village stood in a continuous row on either side of a very clean street. Here and there was a door, but there were no windows. The walls were a strange mixture of colours; sometimes grey, sometimes brick-coloured, and sometimes dark brown. When he saw these different coloured walls, the word 'blind' first came into the thoughts of the explorer. 'The good man who did that,' he thought, 'must have been as blind as a bat.'

Strange people

He climbed down a steep place, and so came to a wall which went round the valley. He could see a number of men and women resting on piles of grass in the meadows, and nearer the village some children were lying asleep. Closer to him three men were carrying buckets* along a little path that ran from the boundary wall towards the houses. They were dressed in clothes of llama cloth with boots and belts of

*llama, a South American animal, used to carry goods.
*bucket, an open container for carrying liquids.

leather. They walked slowly, one behind the other, like men who had been working all night. After waiting for a moment Nunez went forward and gave a loud shout that echoed round the valley.

The three men stopped and moved their heads as though they were looking round them. But they did not appear to see him, and after a while Nunez shouted again, and then once more. And again the word 'blind' came into his thoughts. 'The fools must be blind,' he said to himself.

The three stood side by side, not looking at him, but with their ears directed towards him, judging him by his unfamiliar steps. They stood close together like men a little afraid; and he could see their eyelids were tightly closed. There was an expression of wonder on their faces.

'A man,' one said, ' — a man or a ghost — coming down from the rocks.'

But Nunez advanced with the confident steps of a youth who has just begun to live his life in the way he wishes. All the old stories of the lost valley and the Country of the Blind were coming back to his mind, and through his thoughts came this old saying:

'In the Country of the Blind, the One-eyed Man is King.'

And very politely he greeted them. He talked to them, and used his eyes.

'I come from over the mountains,' said Nunez, 'from the country beyond there where men can see.'

'See?' muttered one. 'See?'

'He comes,' said the second blind man, 'out of the rocks.'

They frightened him by all moving towards him at the same time, and each with a hand held out to touch him. He stepped back from the advance of their fingers.

'Come here,' said the third blind man, following him and catching him neatly.

And they held Nunez and felt him all over. They did not speak again until they had finished.

'Careful!' he cried, when one put a finger in his eye. The blind men thought his eyes and his moving eyelids were most unusual things.

They touched them again.

'Let's lead him to the elders,' said one.

'Shout first,' said the second, 'or else the children will be
5 frightened. This is a wonderful occasion.'

So they shouted, and took Nunez by the hand to lead him
to the houses. He took away his hand. 'I can see,' he said; but
as he turned he tripped over a bucket.

'His senses are imperfect,' said the third blind man. 'He
10 trips, and talks unmeaning words. Lead him by the hand.'

'As you like,' said Nunez; and he was led along, laughing.

It seemed they knew nothing about sight.

Well, in good time he would teach them.

The place appeared larger as he got nearer to it, and the
15 mixed-coloured walls of the houses looked even stranger. A
crowd of children and men and women came round him,
holding on to him, touching him with soft gentle hands,
smelling him, and listening to every word he spoke. The
women and the girls, he was pleased to see, had quite beauti-
20 ful faces, even though their eyes were tightly shut. His three
guides kept close to him, and said again and again, 'A wild
man out of the rocks.'

'Bring him to the elders.'

And they pushed him suddenly through a doorway into a
25 room as black as ink, except that at the end there was the
faint glow of a fire. The people crowded in behind him and
so shut out almost all the daylight, and before he could stop
himself he fell over someone's feet. His arm struck the face
of someone else as he went down. He heard a cry of anger,
30 and for a moment he struggled against a number of hands
that had seized him.

'I fell down,' he said; 'I couldn't see in this inky darkness.'

There was a pause as if the persons about him were trying
to understand his words. Then a voice said: 'He's only newly
35 made! He trips when he walks, and mixes words which mean
nothing with his speech.'

'May I sit up?' he asked. 'I will not struggle against you
again.'

They considered this, and let him rise.

Nunez tries to explain sight

The voice of an older man began to question him. Nunez then tried to explain many things to these elders of the Country of the Blind. He tried to explain the great world out of which he had fallen, the sky and mountains and sight and other such wonders. And they did not believe or understand   5
anything he told them. They could not even understand many of his words. For fourteen generations these people had been blind and separated from the world of sight. The names of all the things of sight had disappeared or changed; the story of the outside world was to them a fairy story.   10

Gradually Nunez realized this; and after they had refused to accept his poor attempt to explain sight, he sat listening to their instruction. The oldest blind man explained to him about life and religion. He explained how the world (meaning their valley) had first been an empty hollow in the rocks, and   15
then llamas had come and a few other creatures that had little sense, and then men, and finally angels, whose moving wings you could hear, but whom no one could touch at all. This greatly puzzled Nunez until he thought of the birds.

He went on to tell Nunez how time was divided into the   20
warm and the cold, which are the same as the day and the night for the blind. He said how it was good to sleep in the warm and work during the cold, and he told Nunez that if he had not arrived that morning, everybody in the village of the blind would have been asleep now. He said the night — for   25
the blind call their day the night — was nearly gone, and everyone should go back to sleep. He asked Nunez if he knew how to sleep. Nunez said he did, but that before sleep he wanted food.

They brought him food — llama's milk in a bowl, and   30
rough salty bread — and led him to a lonely place to eat and then to sleep. But Nunez did not sleep at all.

Instead, he sat in the place where they left him, resting his limbs and making plans.

Every now and then he laughed, sometimes with amuse-   35
ment, and sometimes with anger.

'Explaining things to me as if I were a child!' he thought.

'Thinking I've got no senses! They just don't realize that they've been insulting their new king and master who has been sent to them from heaven! I see I must teach them a few things. Let me think — let me think.'

5 He was still thinking when the sun went down.

Nunez has much to learn

He heard a voice calling to him from the village.

'Ya ho there! Come here!'

He stood up smiling. He would now show these people just how useful sight was. They would look for him, but not

10 find him.

'You're not moving,' said the voice.

He laughed silently, and stepped quietly from the path.

'Don't walk on the grass! That's not allowed.'

Nunez had scarcely heard the sound he made himself. He

15 stopped in amazement.

The owner of the voice came running up the path towards him.

He stepped back on to the path. 'Here I am,' he said.

'Why did you not come when I called you?' said the blind

20 man. 'Must you be led like a child? Can you not hear the path as you walk?'

Nunez laughed. 'I can see it,' he said.

'There's no such word as *see*,' said the blind man after a pause. 'Stop being foolish, and follow the sound of my

25 feet.'

Nunez followed, a little annoyed.

'Soon you will discover what I can do,' he said.

'You'll learn,' answered the blind man. 'There's much to learn in the world.'

30 'Has no one told you, "In the Country of the Blind, the One-eyed Man is King"?'

'What is *blind*?' asked the blind man turning towards him.

Four days passed, and on the fifth day the King of the Blind was still a clumsy and useless stranger among his

35 people. He found working and going about at night annoying, and he decided this would be the first thing he would change.

It was wonderful with what confidence these people moved about. Everything, you see, had been made to suit their needs. Each of the paths of the valley was at a constant angle to the others, and it could be recognized by a special cut in the stone edge. Anything they might trip over in the paths and meadows had been removed a long time before. Their senses had become extremely good. They could hear and judge the slightest movement of a man thirty yards away — could hear the very beating of his heart. Their sense of smell was extraordinary; they could recognize differences between things as easily as a dog can. Nunez found out just how easy and confident their movements could be, when finally he began to insist that they should accept him as a very important man.

He rebelled only after he had tried persuasion.

He tried at first on several occasions to tell them about sight. He spoke of the beauties of sight, of looking at the mountains, the sky, and the sunrise. They told him there were indeed no mountains at all, but the end of the rocks where the llamas lived was the end of the world. They said his thoughts were evil — for they believed that the roofs of the caves, which were smooth to touch, were the roof of the world. But still he tried to show them the practical value of sight. One morning he persuaded them to let him go a long way up the sloping meadows towards the wall with one of the old men. He promised to describe to the old men everything which happened among the houses. He described all he could see, but he could tell the old men nothing about what he could not see — things which were happening inside the houses and behind them. But it was only these which they wanted to test him on.

It was after the failure of this attempt, and when they laughed at him, that he turned to using force. In rage he seized a spade*, and then he discovered a new thing about himself, that it was impossible for him to hit a blind man.

He hesitated, and found they all knew he had picked up the spade. They stood listening with their ears bent towards him, waiting for him to do something.

*spade, a tool for digging.

'Put down that spade!' said one, and he felt a sort of helpless horror.

He pushed one backwards against a wall, and ran past him and out of the village.

5 He went across one of the meadows, leaving behind him a track through the long grass. Presently he sat down on the edge of one of the paths. Far away he saw a number of men carrying spades and sticks come out of the street of houses, and advance towards him in a curved line along the paths.

10 They came slowly, speaking frequently to one another, and often they would stop to smell the air and listen.

The first time they did this Nunez laughed. But afterwards he did not laugh.

One found his track in the grass, and moved forward

15 feeling his way along it.

For five minutes he watched the slow advance of the blind men, and then he became frightened. He stood up, went a step or so towards the boundary wall, turned, and went back a little way. They all stood in a long curve, still and listening.

20 He also stood still, holding his spade very tightly in both hands. Should he attack them?

He moved along the meadow towards a little doorway in the boundary wall, and immediately he moved they followed him. 'I'll kill them if they touch me,' he said to himself, 'I

25 will, I'll hit them!' He shouted aloud, 'Listen to me, I'm going to do what I like in this valley! Do you hear? I'm going to do what I like and go where I like!'

They were moving towards him quickly now. 'Get hold of him!' cried one. He found himself in the centre of a loose

30 curve of blind men.

'I'll hurt you!' he shouted, crying with anger and fear. 'I swear I'll hurt you. Leave me alone!'

Fright

He began to run, not knowing where to go. He ran from the nearest man, because it would be horrible to hit him. He

35 ran for a wide gap between two of them, but they heard him coming and rushed in to stop him. He leapt forward, and

then saw they would catch him. He raised his spade and swung it at the nearest man, hitting him across the hand and arm. The man fell down with a cry of pain, and Nunez ran through the gap.

Through! And then he was close to the street of houses again where there were more blind men with spades and sticks.

He heard steps behind him just in time, and saw a tall man rushing forward and swinging a stick at the sound of him. In great fear, he threw the spade but missed the man. He turned quickly and ran away, and shouted as he got past another one.

He was extremely frightened. He ran wildly across the meadows. Far away in the boundary wall he saw the little doorway, and set off for it as fast as he could go. He did not even look round at the men following him until he reached the doorway and was through it. He climbed a little way up among the rocks, and lay down trying to get back his breath.

And so his little rebellion came to an end.

He stayed outside the wall of the Valley of the Blind for two nights and days without food and shelter. He thought of ways of fighting and conquering these people, but soon he realized it would be impossible for him to do this. He had no weapons, and now it would be hard to get any.

He tried to find food. He thought he could catch a llama and kill it by hammering it with a stone. But the llamas did not trust him, and spat when he came near them. On the second day he became so frightened that he began to shake and tremble.

Finally he crawled down to the wall, and shouted until two blind men came out of the gate to talk to him.

'I was mad,' he said. 'But I was only newly made.'

They said that was better behaviour.

He said he was wiser now, and was sorry for all he had done.

Then he started to cry, for he was very weak and ill. When they heard him crying they felt he was really sorry for doing wrong.

They asked him if he still thought he could 'see'.

'No,' he said. 'That was foolish. The word means nothing — less than nothing!'

They asked him what was above him.

5   'About ten times the height of a man there is a roof above the world — made of rock — and very, very smooth . . . ' He began to cry loudly again. 'Before you ask me any more, give me some food or I shall die.'

He expected punishment, but the blind people were quite 10 kind. They considered his rebellion as proof of his stupidity and unimportance. They gave him the simplest and heaviest work; and he, seeing no other way of living, did what he was told.

The beautiful Medina

So Nunez became a citizen of the Country of the Blind, 15 and came to know some of its people well. There was Yacob, his master, a kind man until he was annoyed; and there was Medina, who was old Yacob's youngest daughter. Nunez thought she was beautiful. Her closed eyelids seemed as if they might open at any moment. There was a look of tender- 20 ness in her face, and her hair shone like silver in the moon-light.

He talked to her every time he had the opportunity. Very gently he spoke to her of sight. She listened to his descrip-tion of the stars and the mountains and her own sweet 25 beauty. She did not believe, she could only half understand, but she was mysteriously delighted, and it seemed to him that she completely understood.

It was one of her sisters who first told Yacob that Medina and Nunez were in love.

30 From the beginning the people did not want Nunez and Medina to marry because they believed he was not as intel-ligent as they were. Her sisters were against the marriage also· because they thought it would bring shame to them all. Old Yacob, although he had begun to like his clumsy, obedient 35 servant, shook his head and said that marriage was impossible.

'You see, my dear,' he said to Medina, 'he's a fool. He can't do anything right.'

'I know,' cried his daughter. 'But he's better than he was. He's getting better. And he's strong, dear father, and kind —
5 stronger and kinder than any other man in the world. And he loves me — and, father, I love him.'

Old Yacob was most unhappy to see her so sad, and so he went and sat in the council-house with the other elders and said, 'He's better than he was. Very likely, some day, we shall
10 find him as clever as we are.'

Then afterwards one of the elders, who was very intelligent, had an idea. He was the great doctor among these people, and he liked the idea of curing Nunez of his unusual behaviour. One day when Yacob was in the council-house
15 the doctor spoke of Nunez again.

Nunez must lose his eyes

'I have examined him,' he said, 'and the problem is now clearer to me. I think very probably he can be cured.'

'That's what I've always hoped,' said old Yacob.

'His brain is damaged,' said the blind doctor. 'Those
20 strange things he calls eyes are diseased, and they have affected his brain. Because of them, his brain is not behaving properly, and is being destroyed slowly.'

'Yes?' said Yacob. 'Yes?'

'And I think I may say that, in order to cure him com-
25 pletely, all we have to do is remove his eyes.'

'And then he won't be mad any more?'

'Then he'll be like everyone else, and an excellent citizen.'

'Thank heaven for science!' said old Yacob, and went home at once to tell Nunez this good news.
30 He was disappointed, however, to find that Nunez was not happy at all when he heard what the old doctor had suggested.

'One might think,' said Yacob, 'from your manner, that you don't love my daughter.'

It was Medina who persuaded Nunez to face the blind
35 doctors.

'*You* do not want me to lose my sight?' he asked her.

She did not answer.

'My world is sight. There are the beautiful things, the beautiful little things — the flowers among the rocks, the sky with its moving clouds, the sunsets and the stars. And there is *you*. It's good to have sight if only to see your beautiful face,   5
and your dear, beautiful hands . . . '

'I wish,' she said, 'sometimes . . . ' She paused.

'Yes?' said he, a little anxiously.

'I wish sometimes — you would not talk like that.'

'Like what?'   10

'I know it's pretty — it's your imagination. I love it, but . . . ' He felt cold. '*But?*' he said faintly.

She sat quite still.

'You mean — you think — it would be better if perhaps I . . . ' He was realizing things very quickly now.   15

'If I were to consent to this?' he said at last, in a voice that was very gentle.

She put her arms round him tightly, 'Oh, if you would,' she cried happily, 'if only you would!'

Freedom

Nunez was unable to sleep for a week before the operation*   20
which was to raise him from his low position in society to being a blind citizen. Sadly he sat or wandered alone while others slept. He had given his answer, he had given his consent, and still he was not sure.

On the last morning he had meant to go to a lonely place   25
where the meadow was beautiful with flowers, and to stay there until it was time for the operation. But as he walked he looked up and went on. He passed through the doorway in the boundary wall and went on towards the rocks, and all the time he was watching the sunlight on the ice and the snow   30
above him.

He saw their great beauty, and he thought of the free outside world — his own world. He thought how after a day or so a man might come down through the mountains, getting nearer and nearer to the busy streets.   35

*operation, the cutting open of the body to remove diseased parts, etc.

For example, if a man went on up that slope to the chimney-way in the rock, then he might come out high among the trees that grew on a sort of shelf. And then? Perhaps he could find a way to climb up the great cliff that 5 came below the snow. And then? Then he would be out upon the snow where the sun was shining, and half-way up to the top of those beautiful mountains.

Nunez glanced back at the village. He thought of Medina, but she had become small and far away.

10   He turned again towards the mountain wall.

Then, very slowly, he began to climb.

The Two Friends

The Prussian Army had reached Paris and was camped all round it. No one could get into the city and no one could leave it, unless he was going to one of the few places on the edge of the city which the French defenders still held. Inside Paris, many of the citizens were extremely hungry. The small birds were gone and even the rats were being caught and eaten. 5

One bright morning Monsieur* Morissot, a clockmaker, was walking sadly along one of the lonely streets. His suit was worn and his stomach was empty. Suddenly he stopped. In front of him stood a man whom he remembered as an old friend. It was Monsieur Sauvage, a merchant, who often used to go fishing with him on Sunday mornings. 10

Before the war started Morissot used to set out from home every Sunday at dawn, carrying a fishing-rod and a tin box hanging over his back. He used to catch a train, get out at Colombes and walk to a part of the river opposite a little island. 15

As soon as he reached this place, which he used to think about all through the week, he would start fishing. He would fish until night came and it was too dark for him to see. It was there he had first met fat, short, cheerful Monsieur Sauvage, who also loved to fish. Usually they would spend the whole of Sunday together on the river bank, sitting with their rods in their hands and their feet hanging over the water. On some days they sat silently and on others they talked, but they understood one another very well without the need for words. You see, they had the same interests and held similar opinions on all important problems. 20 25

Sometimes, on spring mornings, as the sun was beginning to feel warm on their backs and little clouds of mist were rising from the calm water, Morissot would remark, 'Isn't it 30

*Monsieur, is the French word for 'Mister.'

a beautiful day?' And Sauvage would reply, 'Yes, perfect,' —
and they did not have to say another word to understand and
respect one another. Then towards the end of each year, late
in the autumn afternoons as the sun was going down, the
trees on the river bank would tremble at the first touch of   5
winter, their leaves now all red and gold. At such times
Sauvage would smile at Morissot and say, 'What a perfect
evening!', and Morissot, while still fishing carefully, would
answer, 'Yes, better than the streets of Paris.'
    But all that was before the war.   10
    Now, in the empty and lonely Paris street, they greeted
one another sadly. Sauvage sighed. 'What a terrible time this
is!' he said.
    'But what a wonderful day!' replied Morissot unhappily.
'The best day so far this year.' There was not a cloud in the   15
sky, which shone a deep, wonderful blue.
    They wandered along together, each thinking of the happy
days before the war.
    Morissot said, 'Do you remember the days we went fishing?
What happy days they were!'   20
    'Indeed they were. But when will they return again?'

The friends go fishing

    They went into a small restaurant and had some coffee,
and later they continued their walk along the street. The sun
was warm and the soft wind kissed their cheeks. The warm
fresh air made Sauvage excited, and suddenly he stopped and   25
said to his companion, 'Shall we go?'
    'Go? Where?'
    'Go fishing, of course, near our little island. Our soldiers
aren't far from there. I know the officer in charge at
Colombes. I'm sure he'll give us permission.'   30
    Morissot almost trembled with eagerness. 'Yes!' he cried.
'A wonderful idea. I'll come.' So immediately they went
home to get their rods and other fishing equipment.
    An hour or so later they were walking quickly along the
main road out of Paris. They passed many soldiers, dirty,   35
wounded, and tired, and after a while they reached Colombes.

The weary officer smiled a little when they told him what they wanted, and he agreed to let them go. He told them the password* which they would need to get back past the French soldiers.

5   They hurried on again and at last came to a place where there were no more soldiers, not far from their fishing place opposite the little island. All was quiet. On the other side of the river all seemed still. There were some low hills in the distance, and a wide plain which came down to the river.
10   Everything was silent and empty.

Sauvage pointed towards the hills. 'The Prussians are over there,' he said.

Then suddenly, because of that lonely and silent place, they began to feel frightened. Prussians! For months every-
15   one had talked about nothing else. Nobody had ever seen them, but all this time they had been round Paris, moving closer, waiting for hunger to defeat the Frenchmen. In the country areas near Paris, it was said, they stole and murdered. They set fire to and destroyed all the farms, the buildings and
20   the crops after they had taken all they wanted for themselves. Nobody in Paris had seen them; but nobody, it was reported, could resist them, and no one whom they captured could hope to live.

Monsieur Sauvage and Monsieur Morissot looked around
25   carefully. Their legs began to tremble and they held their fishing-rods tightly as if they were prepared to use them as weapons.

'If some of them found us,' whispered Morissot, 'what would happen?'

30   Sauvage, who had just enough courage for a joke, said, 'We would ask them to come fishing with us!'

They stood watching with eyes wide open, and listening with great attention. All was silent; all was still. At last, Sauvage gained some courage.

35   'Come, let's go on, but take care.'

With a final glance around them, they ran quickly across the field that was between them and the river bank. Then,

*password, a secret word which proves to a guard that you are a friend, not an enemy.

out of breath, they jumped into some long grass to hide themselves. Morissot listened in case anyone was moving near them. But no, he heard nothing. They were alone.

They felt more confident now, and began to fish. First Sauvage felt a fish on his hook and then Morissot felt one. *5* After that they were pulling fish out of the water as fast as they could go. Because of the war, nobody had been fishing in the river, and so now there were lots of fish. The two friends had never caught so many before.

They put the fish into a net sack which they had placed *10* half in and half out of the water, and as the sack began to fill up with the delicious little creatures, the fishermen felt an excitement which they thought they would never have felt again.

Suddenly there was a sound like thunder which made the *15* ground tremble. It was the big guns. Over to the left they could see white gun smoke. Sauvage looked round nervously as the guns continued to roar and they could see more and more white smoke. Then he said, 'There they go again,' and he sounded less afraid. *20*

Morissot, who was still fishing, suddenly felt angry with those fools who spent their time fighting and killing one another. 'How foolish men are,' he complained. 'They're like wild animals.'

To which Sauvage replied, 'Of course they are. But while *25* there are governments nothing will ever get better.'

So quickly they began to discuss and solve the political problems of the time. As the guns roared, wounding and killing men and destroying houses, the two friends sat, and fished, and discussed the madness of war. *30*

Captured!

Suddenly they heard the sound of footsteps and they jumped in alarm. Turning, they saw four men, four large men in uniforms, pointing guns at them. The fishing-rods fell from their hands and floated off down the river.

In a few minutes they were tied up with ropes, pushed into *35* a boat, and taken across to the island in the middle of the river. They had thought there was no one there but now they saw about twenty Prussian soldiers. An enormous officer with a beard was leaning on the back of a chair, smoking a pipe. He spoke excellent French.

5   'Well, gentlemen, have you had a good morning's fishing?'

He made a sign, and one of the soldiers put the sack of fish down at his feet.

The Prussian officer smiled. 'Yes, I see you've done quite well. Now, listen to me, for I've some urgent matters to dis-
10   cuss with you. I think you two are spies sent by the French to watch me. To disguise your real purpose, you pretended to fish. Now I've captured you; which is bad luck for you, but that is one of the fortunes of war. As you've got past the French guards you must know the password. Tell it to me. If
15   you refuse, I shall shoot you.'

The two friends stood side by side, frightened and pale. Their hands shook; but they kept silent.

'All right. If you tell me, I'll even let you go. Nobody will know. It'll be your secret. You'll go back as if nothing had
20   happened. But if you refuse, you'll die at once. Make your choice.'

They stood without moving, without saying a word. The officer pointed to the river. 'You must understand that in five minutes you'll be at the bottom of the river – in five
25   minutes – unless you tell me the password. Your families will miss you.'

The two remained silent. The guns continued to thunder in the distance.

The Prussian gave an order, then moved his chair away
30   from the prisoners. Twelve soldiers, with their guns ready, formed a line twenty feet away. He said: 'I'll give you one minute to tell me the password, and no more!'

Then, suddenly, he got up. He went over to Morissot, and taking his arm, led him a few yards away. 'Come,' he
35   whispered, 'tell me the password quickly. Your friend need never know you told me.'

But Morissot said nothing.

The Prussian then went to Sauvage and whispered the same thing.

Sauvage did not reply. Again the friends were put side by side.

A brave death

The order was given. The soldiers aimed their guns. Accidentally, Morissot glanced at the sack of fish lying near them on the grass. He felt weak and his eyes filled with tears.

'Goodbye, Monsieur Sauvage,' he whispered.

'Goodbye, Monsieur Morissot.'

They stood for a moment hand in hand, trembling.

The officer shouted: 'Fire!'

The twelve guns fired together. Sauvage fell forward, face downwards. Morissot, who was taller, turned as he fell, and dropped across his friend's body. Blood flowed out of the holes in their clothes. The soldiers fetched ropes and stones, which they tied to the feet of the two men. Four of them carried the bodies to the river bank, while the big guns went on firing. They swung them back — 'One! two! three!' — and let them go. The bodies flew through the air; and because of the stones at their feet, they sank immediately. After the splash there were little waves which spread to each bank, and then the water became calm again.

The Prussian officer saw the sack of fish. He picked it up off the grass, laughed, and shouted: 'Here!'

A soldier ran up. The officer threw him the sack of fish and said, 'Tell the cook to prepare these little fish while they're still fresh. They'll make a delicious dinner.'

Then he went back to his chair, and began smoking his pipe again.

The Bear-hunt

We were out on a bear-hunting expedition. My friend had shot at a bear, but only wounded him. There was a little blood on the snow, but the bear had got away.

5   We all met together in a group in the forest to decide whether we ought to follow the bear at once or wait two or three days till he settled down again. We asked the bear-drivers* whether it would be possible to get round the bear that day.

  'No. It's impossible,' said one old man. 'You must let the
10 bear settle down. In five days' time it'll be possible to surround him, but if we went after him now, we'd only frighten him away and he'd never lie down.'

  But a young bear-driver began to argue with the old man. He said it was quite possible to surround the bear now.

15   'On this kind of snow,' he said, 'he won't go far, for he's a fat bear. He'll settle down before evening, or, if not, I can catch up with him on snow-shoes*.'

  My companion did not want to follow the bear and advised waiting. But I said, 'We needn't argue. You do what you like,
20 but I'll follow the track with Demyan. If we get round the bear, we'll mark a circle in the snow where he's lying, and then we can come back for him tomorrow. If we don't find him, it doesn't matter. It's still early and we've nothing else to do today.'

25   And so it was arranged.

  The others went back to the sledges* and returned to the village. Demyan and I took some bread and stayed in the forest.

*bear-driver, a person who, by making lots of noise, makes the bear move towards the hunter so that he can shoot it.
*snow-shoes, frames with leather straps for walking on soft snow.
*sledge, a vehicle with runners (long narrow strips of wood or metal) instead of wheels, used on snow.

The weather was fine, cold and calm; but it was hard work walking through the snow. The fresh snow was deep and soft. It had fallen the day before so that our snow-shoes sank six inches into it, and sometimes more.

The bear's track was easy to follow and we could see what   5
he had been doing. Sometimes he sank to his stomach in the snow and cut it up as he went. At first, while we were under the large trees, we could see his track; but when it went into a thicket*, Demyan stopped.

'We must leave the track now,' he said. 'He's probably   10
settled somewhere here. You can see by the snow that he's been sitting down. Let's leave the track and go round; but we must go quietly. Don't shout or cough, or we shall frighten him away.'

We left the path and turned off to the left. But when we   15
had gone about five hundred yards, there were the bear's marks again right before us. We followed them and they led us to the road. Then we stopped and examined the road to see which way the bear had gone. Here and there in the snow we could see the marks of his feet, and even his long claws.   20
The bear had evidently gone towards the village.

As we walked along the road, Demyan said:

'It's no use watching the road now. We shall see where he's turned off, to right or left, by the marks in the soft snow at the side. He must have turned off somewhere, for he   25
won't have gone on to the village.'

We went along the road for nearly a mile, and then, ahead of us, we saw the bear's track, only it was not going from the road into the forest, but from the forest on to the road!. The claw marks were pointing towards the road.   30

'This must be another bear,' I said.

Demyan looked at it and thought for a while.

'No,' said he, 'it's the same one. He's been playing tricks. He walked backwards when he left the road.'

We followed the track, and discovered Demyan was right!   35
The bear had taken ten steps backwards, and then, behind

*thicket, a great many young trees growing thickly together.

a large fir*, he had turned around and gone straight ahead. Demyan stopped and said:

'Now we're sure to get round him. There's a marsh* in front of us and he must have settled down there. Let's go round.'

We began to walk slowly round through a thicket of young firs. I was very tired by this time, and it had become still more difficult to move along. I was damp with sweat, so I took off my warm coat. And there was Demyan all the time, moving along as easily as a boat. His snow-shoes never caught in anything and never slipped off. He even took my coat and hung it over his shoulders, and still he kept urging me to move faster.

We went on for two more miles and arrived at the other side of the marsh. I was moving very slowly. My snow-shoes kept slipping off and I kept tripping. Suddenly Demyan, who was ahead of me, stopped and waved his arm. When I got to him he bent down and pointed with his hand. 'Do you see the bird over those bushes,' he whispered, ' — the one that's so excited? It can smell the bear. That's where he's hiding.'

We turned off and went for another half-mile, and presently we came to the old track again. We had, therefore, been right round the bear, which was now within the circular track we had just made. We stopped, and I took off my cap and loosened my clothes. I felt as if I was in a steam-bath, for I was covered in sweat. Demyan was warm too, and wiped his face with his sleeve.

'Well, sir,' he said, 'we've done our job and now we must rest.'

A welcome rest

The evening sun already showed red through the forest. We took off our snow-shoes and sat down on them, and got some bread and salt from our bags. First I ate some snow, and then some bread; and the bread tasted so good that I thought I had never had any like it before. We sat there

---

fir, an evergreen tree with leaves like needles.
marsh, an area of wet and soft land.

resting until it began to get dark, and then I asked Demyan
if it was far to the village.

'Yes,' he said. 'It must be about eight miles. We'll go there
tonight, but now we must rest. Put on your fur coat, sir, or
you'll get cold.'   *5*

Demyan flattened down the snow, and then broke some
fir branches to make a bed. We lay down side by side, resting
our heads on our arms. I do not remember how I fell asleep.
Two hours later I woke up when I heard something crack.

I had slept so well I did not know where I was. I looked   *10*
round me. How wonderful! It was like some kind of magnificent hall, all white and glittering. After looking for a few
moments, I remembered we were in the forest, and the
glittering hall was, in fact, the tall trees about us, all covered
in frost* and snow. The stars were shining between the   *15*
branches.

The frost had settled when night came. All the trees were
covered with it, Demyan's coat and mine were white with it,
and it dropped down from the branches. I woke Demyan,
and we put on our snow-shoes and set off. It was very quiet   *20*
in the forest. We heard nothing but the sound of our snow-
shoes in the snow; except when now and then a tree, cracking
from the frost, made the forest echo. We heard the sound of
a living creature only once. Something moved close to us and
then rushed away. I was sure it was the bear, but when we   *25*
went to the place where the sound had come from, we found
only the tracks of some small animals.

We reached the road and walked along it, dragging our
snow-shoes behind us. It was easy to walk now. Our snow-
shoes banged behind us as they slid along the hard snow of   *30*
the road. The snow creaked under our boots. The stars
seemed to be running to meet us as they came and went
through the branches of the trees — now shining, now disappearing. It looked as though the whole sky was moving.

My friend was sleeping when I got back, but I woke him   *35*
and told him we had got round the bear. After we had told

*frost, white powder-like covering of frozen vapour on trees, ground,
roots, etc.

the owner of the hotel to get us bear-beaters for the next morning, we had supper and went to bed.

The hunt begins

I was so tired I could have slept till noon if my companion had not wakened me. I jumped up and saw he was already
5   dressed, and busy doing something to his gun.

'Where is Demyan?' I asked him.

'Gone to the forest, hours ago. He's gone to look after the bear-beaters.'

I washed and dressed, and loaded my guns. Then we got
10 into a sledge and set off.

It was still freezing. All was quiet, and the sun could not be seen. There was a thick mist above us, and the frost covered everything.

After driving about two miles along the road, we came
15 near the forest. We saw a cloud of smoke rising, and soon reached a group of country people, both men and women, holding heavy sticks.

We went up to them. The men sat roasting potatoes and laughing and talking to the women.
20 Demyan was there too; and when we arrived the people got up and he led them away to place them in the circle we had made the day before. They went along in a single line, and there were altogether thirty of them. The snow was so deep we could only see the top half of their bodies. They
25 turned into the forest, and my friend and I went in after them. Although they had made a path through the snow, walking was difficult. However, it was also impossible to fall, because there was a wall of snow on each side of our narrow path.
30 We went on in this way for nearly half a mile, when all at once we saw Demyan coming from another direction — running towards us on his snow-shoes and waving at us to join him. We went towards him, and he showed us where to stand. I went to my place and looked round me.
35 There were some tall fir trees to my left, between which I could see quite a long way. I was just able to see one of the

beaters behind the trees. In front of me there was a thicket
of young firs, about as high as a man, with their branches
bent down and stuck together with snow. Through this
thicket there was a path covered thickly with snow, and it
came straight to where I stood. The thicket continued away   *5*
to my right, and there I could see Demyan showing my
friend where to stand.

I examined both my guns and then considered where I
would stand. Three steps behind me was a tall fir.

'That's where I'll stand,' I thought, 'and then I can lean   *10*
my second gun against the tree.' I moved towards the tree,
sinking to my knees in the snow with each step. I flattened
the snow all round where I was going to stand. I held one
gun in my hand, and the other one, loaded and ready, I
placed against the tree.   *15*

They see the bear

Just as I had finished these preparations I heard Demyan
shouting in the distance:

'He's up! He's up!'

'Up! Up! Up! Ou! Ou! Ou!' shouted the beaters round the
circle.   *20*

'Ay! Ay! Ay!' screamed the women.

The bear was inside the circle, and as Demyan chased him,
the people kept shouting. Only my friend and I stood still
and silent, waiting for the bear to come towards us. As I
stood watching and listening, my heart beat quickly. I   *25*
trembled and held my gun tightly.

'Now, now,' I thought. 'He'll come suddenly. I shall aim
my gun, and he'll fall . . . '

Just then, to my left, I heard something falling on the
snow. I looked between the tall firs, and about fifty yards   *30*
behind them I saw something big and black. I raised my gun
and waited.

'Won't he come any nearer?' I thought.

As I waited I saw him move his ears, turn, and go back.
And then, for a moment I saw all of him. He was a huge   *35*
beast. In my excitement I fired, and I heard the bullet hit

a tree. Looking through the smoke, I saw him retreating into the circle, and disappearing among the trees.

'Well,' I thought. 'My chance has gone. He won't come back to me. Either my friend will shoot him or he'll escape
5 through the line of beaters. Anyway, he won't give me another chance.'

I loaded my gun again, however, and then stood listening. The bear-beaters were shouting all round, but to my right, near where my friend stood, I heard a woman screaming:
10   'Here he is! Here he is! Come here! Come here! Ay! Ay! Ay! Ay!'

Just then I saw Demyan with a stick in his hand, and without his snow-shoes, running along a path towards my friend. He stopped beside him, and pointed at something with his
15 stick. Then I saw my friend aim his gun in the same direction. Bang! He fired.

'There,' I thought. 'He's killed him.'

But my friend did not run towards the bear. Evidently he had missed him.
20   'The bear'll get away,' I thought. 'He'll go back, but he won't come towards me a second time. — But what's that?'

Something was coming towards me at great speed, roaring as it came, and I saw the snow flying up quite near me. Straight in front of me was the bear. He was crazy with fear,
25 and was rushing along the path through the thicket right at me. He was hardly six yards from me, and I could see the whole of him — his black chest and enormous head, which was marked with blood. There he was, coming straight at me and scattering the snow as he came. I could see by his eyes
30 that he had not noticed me, but, mad with fear, he was rushing blindly along. He was running straight for the tree I was standing under. I aimed my gun and fired. He was almost upon me now and I realized I had missed. The bullet had gone past him, and he had not even heard me fire, but still
35 kept charging towards me. I aimed again and fired, almost touching his head with the gun. Bang! I had hit him, but not killed him!

The bear attacks

He raised his head and, bending back his ears and showing his teeth, he came at me.

I jumped to get my other gun, but almost before I had touched it, he was on me. He knocked me over into the snow, and ran on past me. *5*

'Thank God, he has left me,' I thought.

I tried to get up, but something held me down and prevented me from moving.

The bear's speed had taken him past me, but he had turned back and fallen on me with the whole weight of his body. I *10* felt something warm above my face, and then I realized he was drawing my face into his mouth. My nose was already in and I felt his heat, and smelt his blood. He was pressing my shoulders down with his feet so that I could not get free. All I could do was move my head down towards my chest and *15* away from his mouth. I was trying to free my nose and eyes, while he tried to get his teeth into them. Then I felt that he had seized the front of my head just below the hair with his lower teeth, and the flesh under my eyes with his upper teeth, and was now closing his jaws. It was as though my *20* face was being cut with knives. I struggled to get free, while he tried to close his teeth like a dog eating a bone. I managed to twist my face away, but he kept drawing it again into his mouth.

'Now,' I thought, 'my end has come.' *25*

Then I felt the weight lifted. I looked up and saw he had gone. He had jumped off me and run away.

When my friend and Demyan saw the bear knock me down and attack me, they rushed to my rescue. My friend, in his haste, ran into the deep snow and fell down. While he was *30* trying to get up, the bear was biting me. But Demyan, who had a stick, but no gun, rushed along the path shouting:

'He's eating the master! He's eating the master!'

And as he ran, he called to the bear:

'Oh, you fool! What are you doing? Stop it! Stop!' *35*

The bear obeyed him and ran away, leaving me lying in the snow.

When I rose, there was much blood on the snow. However, in my excitement I felt no pain.

My friend had reached us by this time, and the other people were arriving too. They looked at my wound and put snow on it. But I, forgetting about my wound, only asked: 5

'Where's the bear? Which way did he go?'

Suddenly I heard:

'Here he is! Here he is!'

And we saw the bear again running toward us. We seized our guns, but before anyone could fire, he had run past us.   10
He was now extremely angry and wanted to attack me again, but when he saw so many people he ran off. We could see by his tracks that his head was bleeding, and we wanted to follow him. However, because my wounds had become very painful, we went instead to the town to find a doctor.   15

The doctor took good care of me, and soon my wounds began to heal.

A month later we went to hunt that bear again, but I did not get the chance to kill him. He would not come out of the circle, but went round and round growling in a terrible voice.   20

Demyan killed him. The bear's lower jaw had been broken, and one of his teeth had been knocked out by my bullet.

He was a huge creature and had beautiful black fur. He looks very fierce even now, as he stands in the corner of my room. The wounds on my face healed well, and their marks   25
can scarcely be seen.

The Paradise* of Thieves

The great Muscari, the wild and courageous young Italian poet, walked into his favourite restaurant, beside the blue waters of the Mediterranean. Servants, dressed in white, were preparing the tables for an early lunch. The restaurant was
5 surrounded by little orange and lemon trees, and Muscari looked at these with satisfaction.

Muscari had a long nose, and long dark hair. He wore a silk handkerchief around his neck and carried a black cloak. He never travelled without his sword, with which he had won
10 many brilliant fights, or without his mandolin*, with which he had actually played to Miss Ethel Harrogate, the young daughter of an English banker* on holiday. Like a boy, he desired both fame and danger, and especially if he was helping some beautiful woman.

15 The banker and his lovely daughter were staying at the hotel attached to Muscari's restaurant; that was why it was his favourite restaurant. He glanced round the room and saw at once that the English guests had not yet come down from their rooms. The restaurant was still empty. Two priests were
20 talking at a table in the corner; however Muscari, although he was a Catholic, took absolutely no notice of them. But from a seat, almost hidden behind one of the small orange trees, a man got up and came towards him. He was wearing clothes quite different from the poet's.

25 This man was dressed in an English suit, a white shirt with a stiff collar, and a pink tie. But he had a dark Italian face, and Muscari realized that he was an old friend named Ezza, whom he had known at college. Although he had been a brilliant student, this young man had failed as a writer of

*paradise, a place of perfect happiness.
*mandolin, a musical instrument with six or eight strings stretched in pairs on a rounded body.
*banker, a person who is in charge of the business of banking.

plays, as an actor, as a traveller, and as a newspaper writer.
In despair he had now become a tourist guide, and was taking
visitors to see all the interesting places in northern Italy.

'Ezza!' cried the poet in delight, and shook his friend's
hand. 'Well, I've seen you dressed in many kinds of clothes   5
on the stage, but I never expected to see you looking like
an Englishman!'

'These,' answered Ezza, seriously, 'are not only the clothes
of an Englishman, but of the Italian of the future.'

'In that case,' remarked Muscari, 'I admit I prefer the   10
Italian of the past.'

'That's your old mistake, Muscari,' said the courier*,
shaking his head; 'and the mistake of Italy. In the sixteenth
century we Italians had the newest steel and the newest
chemistry. Why should we not now have the newest factories,   15
the newest motors — and the newest clothes?'

'Because they are not worth having,' answered Muscari.
'You cannot force Italians to really make progress; they are
too intelligent.'

'Well, to me Marconi is the greatest Italian,' said the other.   20
'That's why I've become a believer in the future — a Futurist
— and a courier.'

'A courier!' cried Muscari, laughing. 'Is that your latest
trade? And whom are you guiding?'

'Oh, a man named Harrogate, and his family.'   25

'Not the banker in this hotel?' inquired the poet eagerly.

'That's the man,' answered the guide.

'Does he pay you well?'

'He will do,' said Ezza, with a slight smile. 'Do you know
he has a daughter — and a son?'   30

'The daughter is like a goddess!' cried Muscari. 'The father
and son are, I suppose, human. But doesn't that banker seem
to you a splendid example of my argument? Harrogate has
millions of pounds, and I have — an empty pocket. He's got
money simply because he collects money, like a boy collects   35
stamps. To be clever enough to get all that money, one must
be stupid enough to want it.'

*courier, a person who is paid to conduct groups of tourists.

'I'm stupid enough for that,' said Ezza. 'Be quiet — here he comes.'

Mr Harrogate, the great banker, did indeed enter the room, but nobody looked at him. He was a tall, rather old man with
5 eyes like pale blue buttons, and he had a small grey beard. He carried several unopened letters in his hand. His son Frank was a really fine young man. He had curly hair and looked healthy; but no one looked at him either. As usual, everyone had turned to look for a moment at Ethel Harrogate, whose
10 pink cheeks, blue eyes and golden hair gave her the appearance of a Greek goddess. The poet Muscari took a deep breath as if he was drinking something, which indeed he was — her beauty, with his eyes. Ezza looked at her too, but in a strange way.

The King of Thieves
15   The Harrogate family were very excited about news of danger on the mountain road they were going to travel on that week. The danger was not from cliffs or landslides, but from something much more exciting. Ethel had been told that robbers still lived in the mountains, and that they attack-
20 ed travellers in lonely places.

'They say,' she cried, with the excitement of a schoolgirl, 'that those mountains aren't ruled by the King of Italy, but by the King of Thieves! Who is the King of Thieves?'

'A great man,' replied Muscari, 'who has become in ten
25 years the terror of the district. Montano, King of Thieves, nails his terrible notices to the trees in every mountain village.'

'Now that sort of thing,' said the banker, 'would never be allowed to happen in England. And perhaps, after all, we
30 should not travel on that road. However, our guide thinks it's perfectly safe.'

'It is perfectly safe,' said Ezza, scornfully, 'I've been on it twenty times. There are no brigands* in the mountains nowadays; they were all captured years ago!'
35   'Nonsense!' cried Muscari. 'A brigand like Montano can

*brigand, a robber who attacks travellers, and usually in lonely places like forests and mountains.

never be captured! Six times the Italian Government tried to
take him from his mountains, and six times the police were
defeated!'

'Oh, it all seems rather frightening,' said the girl, turning
her magnificent eyes towards Muscari. 'Do you really think   *5*
the mountain road is dangerous?'

Muscari raised his noble head proudly. 'I know it's dangerous,' he said. 'I am going to travel on it tomorrow!'

The young Frank Harrogate was left behind for a moment
lighting a cigarette, while his beautiful sister walked into the   *10*
hotel garden with the banker, the courier and the poet. At
the same time the two priests in the corner rose; the taller
one, a white-haired Italian, went out. The shorter priest turned and walked towards the banker's son, who was surprised
to see that he was also an Englishman.   *15*

'You are Mr Frank Harrogate, I think,' he said. 'I will not
introduce myself because it's better that a stranger should tell
you the unusual thing I'm going to say now. Mr Harrogate, I
will say one word and go: take care of your sister in her great
sorrow.'   *20*

Frank Harrogate stared at the little man in amazement. His
sister was extremely happy! He could in fact hear her laughing in the hotel garden.

'Do you mean the brigands?' he asked; and then, remem-
bering something which had been worrying him a little, he   *25*
said, 'Or is it Muscari you mean?'

'One is never thinking of the real sorrow,' said the priest.
'One can only be kind when it comes.'

And he walked quickly from the room, leaving the other
still looking amazed.   *30*

Danger

A day later a coach* carrying the group was moving slowly
and uncomfortably up the road of the high mountains. Ezza
still argued that there was no danger, but Muscari insisted
that there was. In fact, the reason why he had come with

*coach, a four-wheeled vehicle pulled by four or more horses.

them was because he loved danger. The little English priest was also in the coach. He told them he had to cross the mountains that day on business. But young Harrogate could not help thinking that it was the little priest's fears and warn-
5   ings which had made him accompany them. And because of the danger of meeting the thieves, Frank had decided to carry a gun. Even the courier was carrying one. Muscari (with a great sense of pleasure) carried a short sword under his black cloak.

10   He had quickly taken a seat beside the lovely Ethel Harro-gate. On the other side of her sat the English priest, whose name was Brown, and who was fortunately a silent person. The father and son were together on the opposite seat. The courier sat in front driving the coach.

15   They climbed higher and higher. Behind them were the brown fields, but ahead the rocks stood high and wild. At last they came under the huge cliffs which spread out like great wings above a dangerous bend in the narrow road. The horses were frightened by the dark shadow of the cliffs across
20   the road, and refused to go forward. Two of them stood up on their back legs, and although Ezza used his whip, he could not control them. Their sudden movements unbalanced the coach, and all at once it turned over and crashed through a line of bushes and went over the cliff. Muscari immediately
25   put his arms around Ethel to protect her, and he shouted aloud. It was moments like these of danger and excitement that the poet loved more than anything.

Just as they rolled off the mountain road, something very surprising happened. The old banker, Harrogate, jumped out
30   of the coach and leapt over the cliff before the falling vehicle could take him there. At first it seemed as if he was trying to kill himself, but then it was clear he had acted sensibly. Evidently the man had more energy and more wisdom than Muscari had thought he had, for he landed safely on a piece
35   of soft ground, which could almost have been put there for him to fall on!

The whole group in fact were equally lucky. Just below this part of the road there was a small flat meadow in a hollow, and they fell into it without hurting themselves. However, some of their luggage burst open, and the contents of their pockets spilled out in the grass all about them. But the coach was wrecked, and the horses were lying painfully beside it.   5

The first to sit up was the little priest, who glanced about him with a look of foolish wonder on his face. Frank Harrogate heard him say to himself: 'Now, why have we fallen just here?'

Among the things scattered in the grass were Muscari's   10
wide hat, and beyond it, a fat, unopened business envelope which, after a look at the address, the priest returned to its owner, the elder Harrogate. On the other side of him the grass and flowers partly hid Ethel's umbrella. This he took back to the girl, whom Muscari was then helping to stand up.   15
'We have fallen into heaven,' said the poet. 'Humans climb up and they fall down; but it's only gods and goddesses who can fall upwards!'

When Muscari had lifted the lady from the ground he bowed to her, and then turned to help the horses. Using his   20
sword he cut them free of the wrecked coach, and soon they were standing in the grass, trembling.

Brigands

After he had finished, a remarkable thing happened. A quiet man, his face dark brown from the sun and wind, and wearing old and worn clothes, came out of the bushes and   25
took hold of the horses' heads. He had an unusual looking knife, very broad and crooked, in his belt. Muscari asked him who he was, and he did not answer.

The poet looked around him at the shocked and frightened group in the hollow, and then he saw another silent man,   30
with a gun under his arm, who was looking at them from the bushes on the other side. Next he looked up at the road and saw, looking down at them, the barrels of four other guns and four other brown faces with bright but unmoving eyes.

'The brigands!' cried Muscari, with delight. 'This was a   35
trap. Ezza, get out your gun! There are only six of them. Put

the lady in the middle, and we'll break through that line of
them up there — with a rush.'

And pushing through the tall grass and flowers, he advanced fearlessly towards the four guns. But finding no one
followed him except young Harrogate, he turned, waving his   *5*
sword above his head to bring on the others. He saw the
courier still standing, feet apart, in the centre of the hollow,
with his hands in his pockets.

'You thought, Muscari, that I was a failure among our college friends,' he said, 'and you thought you were successful.   *10*
But I've succeeded more than you, and I'll have a bigger place
in history. I've been doing brave deeds while you've only
been writing about them!'

'Come on, I tell you!' shouted Muscari. 'Will you stand
there talking nonsense about yourself when there's a woman   *15*
to save and two strong men to help you? What kind of a man
do you call yourself?'

'I call myself Montano!' cried the strange courier, equally
loud and strong. 'I'm the King of Thieves, and I welcome you
all to my mountain kingdom!'   *20*

And while he spoke, five more silent men with weapons
ready came out of the bushes, and waited for him to give
them orders. One of them held a large notice.

The Paradise of Thieves

'This pretty place,' the courier-brigand went on, 'together
with some caves underneath it, is called the Paradise of   *25*
Thieves. It's my principal stronghold* in these mountains, for
it cannot be seen from the road above, or from the valley
below.'

The King of Thieves smiled sternly at them all, and then
continued to speak in the same polite and yet frightening   *30*
way.

'Now for my plans. Some of you I shall hold for ransom*
but Father Brown and the famous Muscari I shall let go free
tomorrow at dawn. Priests and poets, if you will excuse me

stronghold, a place which is easy to defend against attack.
ransom, the money which is paid to free a prisoner.

for saying it, never have any money, and therefore it's impossible to get any from them.'

The King of Thieves now took the large notice from the waiting brigand and, after reading it quickly and silently,
5   went on:

'My other intentions are clearly written here in this notice, copies of which will be nailed on a tree in every village in the valley, and at every crossing place in the mountains. In it I announce first that I've captured the rich Englishman, the
10   great banker, Mr Samuel Harrogate. I next announce that I've found in his pockets two thousand pounds, which, Mr Harrogate, you will now give to me.'

The banker looked at him from under his eyebrows, and his face was red with anger. However, he was not going to dis-
15   obey the robber. That leap from the coach seemed to have used up all his strength. His trembling hand went slowly to his pocket, and he handed the brigand the fat envelope which Father Brown had seen earlier on the grass.

'Excellent!' cried the robber. 'Now the third thing in my
20   notice is about ransom. I'm asking for three thousand pounds from the friends of Mr Harrogate's family. And I must also tell you that the notice ends with details of the very unpleasant things which may happen to you if the money is not paid. But in the meantime, let me assure you all that you'll
25   be comfortable and well cared for. I can offer you a place to sleep which is dry and warm, and also an excellent meal with wine and cigars. So welcome, for the present, to the luxuries of the Paradise of Thieves!'

When at last he realized he could do nothing, Muscari put
30   his sword back under his cloak and sat down angrily on the long grass. The girl had gone over to comfort her father. Now the priest came towards him and sat down quite close to him. Muscari spoke to him crossly:

'Well!' he said, 'do people still think I'm foolish, or do
35   they now agree that there are still brigands in the mountains?'

'There may be,' said Father Brown, mysteriously.

'What do you mean?'

'I mean that I'm puzzled,' replied the priest. 'I'm puzzled

about Ezza or Montano, or whatever his name is. He seems to me much more strange as a robber than even he was as a courier.'

'But in what way?' the poet asked. 'Indeed, I should have thought the robber was plain enough.'

'I notice three difficulties,' said the priest quietly, 'and I should like to have your opinion of them. First of all I must tell you that I was having lunch in the restaurant at the hotel, and I noticed something. As four of you left the room, you and Miss Harrogate went ahead, talking and laughing. The banker and the courier walked behind, speaking rather softly. But, I heard Ezza say these words — "Well, let her have a little fun; you know the blow may smash her at any minute." I therefore warned her brother that she might be in some kind of danger; but just what kind, I have no idea. However, if it meant this capture in the mountains, then it doesn't make any sense. Why should Ezza warn the banker, even in so slight a way, of the trap he was planning? So, it couldn't have meant that. But if not, then what is the other danger to Miss Harrogate, which the courier and the banker know about?'

'Danger to Miss Harrogate!' cried the poet, fiercely. 'Explain to me; go on!'

'All these puzzles have something to do with our robber chief,' went on the priest thoughtfully. 'And here is the second of them. Why did he announce in his demand for ransom the fact that he'd already taken two thousand pounds from his victim? This won't encourage Harrogate's friends to pay the ransom. It might stop them in fact. They're far more likely to think Harrogate would be in greater danger if the thieves were poor and in great need of money. Why should Ezza want so specially to tell all Europe that he'd robbed the banker before demanding the ransom?'

'I can't imagine,' said Muscari. 'You may think you're helping me to understand, but you're making me more confused. What's the third puzzle concerning the King of Thieves?'

'The third puzzle,' said Father Brown, talking more to

himself than to Muscari, 'is this field we're sitting in. Why does our courier-robber call this his main stronghold and the Paradise of Thieves? It's certainly a soft place to fall on and a pretty place to look at. It's also quite true, as he says, that it can't be seen from the road or the valley, and is therefore a good hiding-place. But, I think it would be the worst stronghold in the world. It could easily be attacked from the road above — the actual place where the police would most probably pass. A few big guns from the road could blow this meadow right over the cliff. No, it's not a stronghold; it's something else. If it has some importance, then I don't understand what that importance is. Why it's more like a theatre without a roof — a stage or a scene for a funny play. It's like . . .'

Rescue

As the little priest's words went on and on, Muscari suddenly began to hear a new noise in the mountains. The noise was very small and faint; but the light evening wind seemed to be carrying the sound of horses and shouting from the distance.

At the same moment, Montano the robber ran up the bank and stood in the bushes, staring down the road. The thieves began to hide themselves among the trees and bushes as the noise of the horses grew louder. A voice could be heard calling out orders.

'Rescue!' shouted Muscari, jumping to his feet and waving his hat. 'The police and soldiers are here! Now we'll fight these brigands. Follow me!'

And throwing his hat away over the trees, he pulled out his sword once more and began to climb the slope to the road. Frank Harrogate jumped up and ran across to help him, but he was suprised to hear his father calling him back.

'I won't allow it!' cried the banker in a choking voice. 'I command you not to interfere.'

'But father,' said Frank, angrily, 'an Italian gentleman has led the way. Do you want people to say an Englishman was afraid to follow?'

'It's useless,' said the older man, who was trembling violently, 'it's useless. We must accept what's going to happen.'

Father Brown looked at the banker, and all at once he understood everything.

Meanwhile, Muscari had reached the road. He struck the King of Thieves so hard on the shoulder that he nearly fell. Montano also had a sword ready; but even as the two blades crossed, he stopped fighting and laughed.

'What's the use, my friend?' he said, happily. 'This silly play-acting will soon be over.'

'What do you mean, you devil?' cried the excited poet. 'Have you lost your courage as well as your honesty?'

'Everything about me is false,' Ezza replied, laughing. 'I'm an actor, but I'm neither a real thief nor a real courier. I'm just a man playing tricks, so it would be stupid to fight with me.' And he laughed like a happy schoolboy, and sat down on the grass with his back to the road, where they could now see the soldiers on their horses.

Muscari stood in the growing darkness, for once silent in wonder. Then he noticed the strange little priest standing beside him and talking to him.

'My friend,' the priest said in a low voice, 'you must forgive me asking you a private matter at such a time; but do you care about the girl? Care enough to marry her and be a good husband to her, I mean?'

'Yes,' said the poet, quite simply.

'Does she care about you?'

'I think so,' was the equally serious reply.

'Then,' said the priest, 'go to her at once and ask her to marry you. There's not much time.'

'Why?' asked Muscari, in amazement.

'Because,' said Father Brown, 'there's great danger coming up the road for her.'

'Nothing's coming up the road,' argued Muscari, 'except the rescue.'

Almost as he spoke, the brigands began to run from the bushes. They rushed through the long grass like sheep running away from dogs, as they tried to escape from the sol-

diers. Then through a gap in the bushes, came an officer with a small grey beard. He had a piece of paper in his hand, and he walked right into the centre of the Paradise of Thieves. Seeing the King of Thieves sitting in his way, he gave him a
5 push which knocked him over. 'You'll get into trouble, too,' he said, 'if you play any more tricks!'

Who is the real brigand?

This seemed to Muscari scarcely like the capture of a great and dangerous brigand. Going on, however, the officer stopped in front of the three Harrogates and said: 'Samuel Harro-
10 gate, I arrest you on the orders of the English police for stealing and spending money belonging to your bank.'

The anger of the Italian officer, when he later explained the affair to Father Brown, was mixed with admiration for the elder Harrogate.
15 'At least *he* was a great brigand,' he said. 'He ran away with the bank's money to Italy. Here he arranged to have himself captured by men pretending to be brigands, so as to explain why both the money and himself had disappeared. But for years he's been doing things as clever as that, quite as
20 clever as that.'

Muscari took away the unhappy daughter, who stayed close by him then, and in the years that followed. But even in that unhappy moment in the little green hollow, he could not help laughing at the unfortunate Ezza.
25 'And where are you going next?' he asked him.

'Birmingham,' answered the actor, as he lit a. cigarette. 'Didn't I tell you I was a Futurist? I really do believe in those things if I believe in anything. Change, progress and new things every morning. I'm going to Manchester, Glasgow,
30 Chicago — that is, to intelligent, energetic, and civilized society!'

'That is,' said Muscari, 'to the real Paradise of Thieves.'

'Blow Up with The Ship!'

I have got a rather frightening confession to make. I am haunted* by a ghost.

If you were to guess for a hundred years, you would never guess what my ghost is. I shall make you laugh now — and afterwards I shall make you very, very, frightened. My Ghost   5
is the ghost of a Kitchen Candlestick.*

I may not be the cleverest man in the world, but I think that the haunting of any man with any thing begins with the frightening of him. Anyway, the haunting of me with the kitchen candlestick and candle began with the frightening of   10
me with a kitchen candlestick and candle — frightening me until I went mad.

Here are the details of my story as well as I can describe them.

I was sent off to be a sailor when I was still a boy, and I   15
became a mate* when I was twenty-five. It was in the year 1818, when the Spanish colonies in South America were fighting for their freedom. There was plenty of blood flowing between the Government of Spain and the rebels, who were led by General Bolivar — a famous man at that time, though   20
people don't seem to remember him now. Many Englishmen and Irishmen went to fight with the General; and some of our merchants sent him supplies across the ocean.

I was then the mate of a ship belonging to a certain merchant in London who sent the ship, in the year I am speaking   25
of, with a cargo of gunpowder* for General Bolivar and his men. Nobody knew anything about our instructions when we sailed, except the captain; and he didn't seem to like them. I

*to be haunted, to be visited by the ghost of someone or something frequently.
*candlestick, a holder for a candle.
*mate, a ship's officer below the captain.
*gunpowder, powder which explodes; used in bullets, fireworks, etc.

can't say how many barrels of gunpowder we had, or how much was in each barrel — I only know we had no other cargo. The name of the ship was the *Good Intent** — a strange name for a ship carrying gunpowder, and sent to help a
5 revolution.

The *Good Intent* was the craziest old ship I ever sailed in. She was quite large and had a crew of eight — not really enough men to sail her well. However, we were paid good wages; and we had to balance that against the risk of sinking
10 in a storm — and also, on this voyage, against the risk of being blown up.

Because of our dangerous cargo, we had some new regulations, which we didn't like at all, against smoking our pipes and lighting our lamps. But, as usual in such cases, the cap-
15 tain, who made the rules, didn't obey them himself. None of us was allowed to have a lighted candle in his hand when he went down to his cabin — except the captain; and he used to light his, just as usual, when he went down to his cabin, or when he went to look at the maps on the cabin table.
20 This light was an ordinary kitchen candle, and it stood in an old, flat candlestick, with all the paint worn and melted off, and all the tin showing through. It would have been more suitable and safer if he had had a lamp; but he kept to his old candlestick. And that same old candlestick has ever since
25 kept to *me*!

Waiting for a signal
We steered first for the Virgin Islands in the West Indies, and as soon as we saw them, we sailed off towards the Leeward Islands. Then we went straight south until we saw land. That land was the coast of South America. We had had a
30 wonderful voyage. We had lost no sails or any other equipment, and none of us had had to work the ship's pumps. It wasn't often the *Good Intent* had such a good voyage.

The captain went to his cabin, and read his letter of instructions and looked at the map. When he came on deck he
35 told us to steer away from the land. It was dark before he
intent, as used in this story, it has the same meaning as 'intention.'

brought us close to the coast again. None of us knew how the
currents ran on that coast. We all wondered why he didn't
anchor the ship; but he said no, he must first signal with a
light, and then must wait for an answering light from the
beach. We waited, but nothing appeared. It was a clear, calm   5
night with bright stars. What little wind there was came
gently from the land. I suppose we waited, moving a little to
the west, for almost an hour before anything happened — and
then, instead of seeing a light on the beach, we saw a boat
coming towards us, rowed by two men.   10

We asked them who they were and they answered
'Friends!' and called us by our name. They came on board.
One of·them was an Irishman, and the other was an evil-
looking native pilot, who spoke only a little English.

The Irishman handed a note to our captain, who showed it   15
to me. It informed us that the part of the coast we were near
was not safe for unloading our cargo, because spies of the
enemy (that is to say, the Spanish Government) had been
captured and shot in the area the day before. It also told us
to trust the native pilot, who had instructions to take us to   20
another part of the coast. The note was signed by the proper
officials; so we let the Irishman go back alone in the boat,
and allowed the pilot to take charge of the ship. He kept us
sailing away from the land till noon the next day — his instructions, evidently, were to keep the ship out of sight of   25
land. We only altered our direction in the afternoon, so as
to come close to the land a little before midnight.

The pilot was about the most evil-looking man I had ever
seen. He was thin, cowardly, and always angry; and he swore
at the men in the very worst English till every one of them   30
wanted to throw him into the sea. The captain and I kept
them quiet. When it was nearly dark, however, I was unlucky
enough to quarrel with him.

He wanted to go to his cabin to smoke his pipe, and I
stopped him, of course, because of the regulations. He tried   35
to push by me, so I pushed him away with my hand. I never
meant to knock him down, but somehow I did. He got up as
quick as lightning, and pulled out his knife. Just as quickly,

I pulled it from his hand, hit him across his ugly face, and threw his weapon into the sea. He looked at me with hatred, and then walked away.

5   We came close to the land again between eleven and twelve that night, and anchored.

It was very dark and very quiet. The captain was on deck with two of our best men. The rest were in their cabins, except the pilot, who was lying on the deck, looking more like a snake than a man. It was not my turn for duty until
10   four in the morning. However, I was a bit worried about a few things, such as the weather, the pilot, and the state of affairs generally, so I lay on the deck to get some sleep, and also to be ready in case anything happened. The last thing I remember was the captain whispering to me that he was
15   worried too, and that he would go to his cabin to read his instructions again. That is the last thing I remember before the slow, regular roll of the ship sent me off to sleep.

Murder

I was awakened by the noise of fighting, and then someone put a gag* in my mouth. There was a man on my chest and a
20   man on my legs, and they tied my hands and feet in half a minute.

The Spaniards now had control of the ship. They were all over her. I heard six heavy splashes in the water, one after the other. I saw them kill the captain with a knife as he came
25   running up the deck, and then I heard a seventh splash. Except for myself, all the crew had been murdered and thrown into the sea. I couldn't think why they had left me until I saw the pilot lean over me with a lamp, and look to make sure who I was. He looked as evil as the devil, and he
30   shook his head at me as if to say, *You* were the man who knocked me down and hit my face, and now I'm going to play a nasty little game of revenge with you!

I could neither move nor speak, but I could see the Spaniards take off the covers so that they could get up the cargo.

*gag, something put over a person's mouth to keep him quiet.

A quarter of an hour later I heard the oars of a small boat in the water near the ship. The Spaniards began to unload the cargo into her. They all worked hard except the pilot, and he came from time to time, with his lamp, to have another look at me, and to laugh at me in that evil way of his. I am old *5* enough now not to be ashamed of confessing the truth, so I don't mind admitting that the pilot frightened me. He was clearly a spy. Either he or his Spanish employers had known enough about us to suspect what our cargo was, and then trap us. But what did he intend to do to me? *10*

It makes me shake with fear, even now, to tell you what he did with me.

The fright, and the ropes, and the gag, and not being able to move hand or foot, had made me very tired by the time the Spaniards stopped working. This was just as dawn came. *15* They had moved a large part of our cargo on board the boat, but not nearly all of it. They wanted to get away with what they had got before daylight.

After all the rest of them were off the ship, the pilot and two Spanish sailors lifted me up, still with the gag and the *20* ropes, and took me down to the bottom of the ship and put me on the floor. They tied more ropes to me so that I could just turn from one side to the other, but could not roll myself over to change my position on the floor. Then they left me.

I lay in the dark for a short while, with my heart beating *25* fast with fear. I lay like this for about five minutes, and then the pilot returned alone.

He had the captain's old candlestick and some carpenter's tools in one hand, and a long piece of thin rope in the other. He put the candlestick, with a new candle lighted in it, down *30* on the floor about two feet from my face, and very close to the side of the ship. The light was weak; but it was enough to show a dozen barrels of gunpowder left all around me in the bottom of the ship. I began to suspect what he was going to do. I shook from head to foot, and sweat poured off my face *35* like water.

I saw him go to one of the barrels of powder which was about five feet from the lighted candle. He made a hole in the

side of the barrel, and the terrible black powder flowed slowly out. He then rubbed the powder into the piece of thin
rope until it was all black with it. He pushed one end of the
rope into the small hole in the barrel.

5   The next thing he did was to tie the other end of that thin,
black, terrible rope around the lighted candle beside my face.
There was about three inches between the end of the rope
and the little yellow flame.

He did that, and then looked to see if the ropes and the
10   gag in my mouth were all right. Then he stood up and
whispered roughly to me, 'Blow up with the ship!'

He was on deck again a moment after, and he and the two
others closed the deck cover over me. They didn't put it on
properly and at one end there was a small crack, and through
15   this I could see a little daylight. I heard the oars of their boat
fall into the water — splash! splash! fainter and fainter, for a
quarter of an hour or more.

While these sounds were in my ears, my eyes stared at the
candle.

Waiting to die

20   It had not been lit for long. Unless something unusual
happened, the flame would take about two hours to reach
the rope. There I lay, watching the candle burning down, and
knowing my life was burning away with it. There I lay, alone
on the sea, waiting to be blown to little pieces, unable to help
25   myself or call to others for help. The wonder is that I didn't
cheat the flame, the rope, and the powder, and die from
terror in the first half-hour.

I can't say exactly how long I kept control of my senses
after the sound of the oars in the water had disappeared. I
30   can remember everything I did and everything I thought up
to a certain point; but after that point, I lose myself in my
memory, just as I lost myself in my own feelings at that time.

I began by trying to free my hands. Due to the mad fear I
was in, I cut my flesh with the ropes as if they had been knife
35   blades, but I couldn't free my hands. There was less chance
of freeing my legs, or of loosening the ropes which held me

to the floor. I gave up when I got tired from lack of breath. The gag was a terrible enemy to me; I could only breathe through my nose, and so I almost choked.

I stopped struggling and lay quiet, and got back my breath again. But all the time I watched the candle.

While I was staring at it, I thought of a way to blow out the flame by pumping a long breath at it through my nose. But it was too high above me and too far away from me. I tried, and tried and tried; and then I gave up again, and lay quiet again, always with my eyes staring at the candle, and the candle staring back at *me*. I calculated that I had less than an hour and a half to live.

An hour and a half! Was there a chance that in that time a boat would come to the ship from the land? I thought that whoever, rebels or Spaniards, controlled the land near the ship would send out someone to find out why it was anchored there. The question for *me* was, how soon? The sun had not risen yet, which I knew by looking at the crack of daylight. I knew there was no village nearby, because we had seen no lights along the coast. I could tell by listening that there was no wind, and so no strange ship could come near. In other words, because it was so early, because of the uninhabited coast, and because of the calm, there was no chance for me. As I felt that, I had another struggle – the last – with the ropes which held me; but I only cut myself deeper.

An hour and a quarter.

I began to wonder what sort of death blowing up might be. Painful! Surely, it would be too sudden for that? Perhaps just one crash inside me, or outside me, or both; and nothing more! I couldn't decide; I couldn't decide how it would be.

I tried to pray – in my heart, for the gag stopped me praying aloud. I tried hard, but the flame seemed to burn away the prayers in my heart. I tried not to look at the candle and its slow, murdering flame, but to look instead at the glorious daylight through the crack in the cover. I tried once, tried twice; and gave it up. Next, I tried to shut my eyes and keep them shut. But I seemed to have no power over them and they opened again, and the flame of the candle flew into them, or so it seemed, and it burned up the rest of my thoughts in an instant.

Madness

I started laughing.

Yes! laughing! I would have screamed with laughter if the gag hadn't stopped me. As it was, I shook with it inside me — shook until the blood was in my head, and until I almost choked from lack of breath. I had just enough sense left to feel that my own terrible laughter at that awful moment was a sign that I was going mad at last.

Then the flame held my eyes as firmly as the ropes held my hands and legs. I couldn't look away from it. I couldn't even shut my eyes, when I tried that again for the second time. There was the flame growing tall. There was the piece of unburned candle between the flame and the gunpowder-rope, which was now only an inch or less.

How much life did that inch leave me? Three-quarters of an hour? Half an hour? Fifty minutes? Twenty minutes? Steady! an inch of candle will burn for more than twenty minutes. Again the mad laughter began. I shook and swelled like a frog and choked myself, till the light of the candle leaped in through my eyes, and forced up the laughter, and burned it out of me, and made me all empty and cold once more.

Suddenly I thought of the pilot, his long thin hands dripping with gunpowder. No! no hands, no gunpowder — nothing but the pilot's face, shining red hot, like the sun, in the mist of fire; turning upside down in the mist of fire; running backwards and forwards in the mist of fire; spinning millions of miles in the mist of fire — spinning smaller and smaller into one tiny point, and that point shooting straight into my head. And then all fire and all mist — no hearing, no seeing, no thinking, no feeling — the ship, the sea, my own self, the whole world, all gone together!

I wake at last

After what I've just told you, I know nothing and remember nothing, till I woke up (as it seemed to me) in a comfortable bed. There were two men sitting, one on each side of my pillow, and a gentleman standing watching me at the end of the bed. It was about seven in the morning.

5   My sleep (or what I think was sleep) had lasted for eight months — I was among English people on the island of Trinidad. The men at each side of my pillow were my nurses, and the man at the end of the bed was my doctor. What I said and did in those eight months I have never known, and never

10   shall. I woke out of it as if it had been one long sleep — that's all I know.

It was another two months or more before the doctor thought it was safe to answer the questions I asked him.

An American ship, waiting for wind near the coast, had

15   seen the *Good Intent* as the sun rose; and the captain, seeing her anchored where no ship had any reason to be, had sent his mate in one of his boats, to find out what was happening.

What he saw, when he and his men arrived on board, was a gleam of candlelight through a crack in the deck. The flame

20   was the width of a hair from the gunpowder-rope when he reached me. If he had not had the sense and courage to blow out the candle at once, he and his men might have blown up with the ship as well as me.

What happened to the Spanish boat and the pilot I have

25   never heard from that day to this.

As for the *Good Intent*, the Americans took her, just as they took me, to Trinidad. I was landed in exactly the same state as when they rescued me — that's to say, in a kind of deep sleep. But please remember, it was a long time ago; and

30   finally I was cured.

My only trouble is, that I'm haunted by that ghost. The ghost of an old, worn Kitchen Candlestick.

The Speckled* Band

I woke one morning early in April, and saw my friend Sherlock Holmes, the famous detective*, standing fully dressed by the side of my bed. He usually got up late, and as the clock on the table beside my bed showed me that it was only a quarter past seven, I looked at him in surprise.

'I'm very sorry to wake you up, Watson,' said he.

'What is it, a fire?'

'No. The servant says a young lady has arrived, and wants to see me immediately. She's waiting now in the sitting-room. Now when young ladies wander about the town at this hour of the morning, and wake sleepy people out of their beds, I think they must have something very urgent to say. If this proves to be an interesting case*, you would, I'm sure, wish to follow it from the beginning. I thought at least that I should give you the chance.'

'My dear man, I wouldn't miss it for anything.'

There is nothing which gives me more pleasure than to follow Holmes in his investigations*, and to admire the way he solves problems. I dressed rapidly, and was ready in a few minutes to accompany my friend to the sitting-room. A lady dressed in black, who had been sitting near the window, rose as we entered.

'Good morning, madam,' said Holmes, cheerfully. 'My name's Sherlock Holmes. This is my friend, Dr Watson, whom you can trust not to speak to anyone about what you tell me. But first I shall order you a cup of hot coffee, for I see you're trembling.'

*speckled, marked with speckles (small spots).
*detective, a person whose job is to discover criminals and solve crimes.
*case, a criminal matter which is being examined by a detective.
*investigation, the examination of a crime.

'It's not cold which makes me tremble,' said the lady, in a low voice.

'What is it, then?'

'It is fear, Mr Holmes. It is terror.'

5 We could see that she was indeed extremely worried. Her face was grey, and her frightened eyes looked like the eyes of a hunted animal. She seemed about thirty, but her hair was turning grey, and she looked very tired.

'You must not be frightened,' said Holmes, gently; and he
10 bent forward to pat her arm. 'We shall soon put matters right, I'm sure. You've come by train this morning, I see.'

'You know me, then?'

'No, but I can see part of the ticket inside your left glove. You must have started early, and you had a dirty drive along
15 rough roads, before you reached the station.'

The lady stared in wonder at my companion.

'There's no mystery,' he said, smiling. 'There's some mud on the left arm of your coat.'

'You're perfectly correct,' said she. 'I started from home
20 before six, and came by the first train. Sir, I want to be free of this terrible fear. I shall go mad if it continues. Oh, sir, do you think you could help me out of my danger? At present I've no money to pay for your services, but in a month or two I shall be married, and then I can pay your fee.'

25 'There's no fee. You've only to pay my travelling expenses, which you can do later. And now, please tell us everything about your trouble.'

'Oh,' replied our visitor, 'the danger I feel is difficult to explain because I've no really good proof — only suspicions.
30 Even the man I'm going to marry thinks my suspicions are just the false ideas of a nervous woman.

'My name's Helen Stoner, and I'm living with my step-father*, who's the last member of one of England's oldest families, the Roylotts of Stoke Moran.'

35 'The name is familiar to me,' said Holmes.

'The family at one time was also one of the richest in England, but my grandfather lost everything by gambling.

*stepfather, a man who is married to the mother of a child, but who is not that child's real father.

Nothing was left except a small piece of land, and the two-hundred-year-old house. His only son, that is, my stepfather, borrowed some money from a relative so that he could study to become a doctor. Later he went to Calcutta to work. In Calcutta he beat his servant to death in a moment of great   5
anger, because something had been stolen from his house. He was lucky that he wasn't hanged for this crime, but he did have to spend many years in prison. When he was free again, he returned to England, but he was now a disappointed and unhappy man.   10

'When Dr Roylott was in India he married my mother, Mrs Stoner. She was the young widow of General Stoner of the Bengal Army. My sister Julia and I were twins*,.and we were only two years old when our mother married Dr Roylott. She had a great deal of money which she gave him when he agreed   15
he would give Julia and me a certain amount every year if we married. My mother died in a railway accident soon after we returned to England. Dr Roylott then took us to live with him in his old home at Stoke Moran. The money which my mother had given him was enough for us to live on.   20

'But at about this time my stepfather began to change. Instead of being friendly with our neighbours and visiting them, he quarrelled with them all, and shut himself up in his house. His violent temper had become worse since he had lived in India. He now got into some disgraceful fights, and   25
was twice in court for causing trouble. At last he became the terror of the village, and the people would run away when they saw him, for he is a man of great strength and fierce anger.

'He's no friends except the wandering gypsies*, whom he   30
lets camp on his land. For this, they let him visit them in their tents, and sometimes he wanders away with them for weeks. He also likes Indian animals. He has a cheetah* and a baboon* which one of his friends sent him. They wander

*twins, two children born together of the same mother.
*gypsy, a member of an Asiatic race who wander in many European
    countries.
*cheetah, an animal of the cat family.
*baboon, a type of large monkey.

freely over his land, and the villagers fear them almost as much as they fear him.

'You can imagine from what I've told you that my poor sister Julia and I lived in misery. No servant would stay with us, and for a long time we did all the work in the house. She was only thirty at the time of her death, and yet her hair was already turning grey, like mine.'

'Your sister is dead, then?' asked Holmes.

'She died just two years ago, and it's about her death that I wish to speak to you. I've an aunt, my mother's sister, Miss Honoria Westphail, and sometimes we were allowed to visit her. Julia went there at Christmas two years ago, and there she met a retired army officer. They decided to get married. My stepfather said he had no objection to the marriage; but within two weeks of the wedding day, a terrible thing happened.'

How did she die?

Sherlock Holmes had been leaning back in his chair with his eyes shut and his head on a soft cushion, but half opened them now, and looked at his visitor.

'Please tell me the details,' he said.

'That's easy,' she replied, 'for they're clear in my memory. The house is, as I've told you, very old, and we use only part of it now. The bedrooms in this part of it are on the ground floor. The first one is Dr Roylott's, the second is my sister's and the third is mine. There are no doors between them, but each has a door which opens into the same corridor*. That's clear enough, I think.'

'Perfectly clear.'

'The windows of the three rooms open out into the garden. That night Dr Roylott had gone to his room early, though we knew he hadn't gone to sleep, for my sister was troubled by the smell of the Indian cigars he likes to smoke. Therefore, she left her room and came into mine, where she sat for some time talking about her wedding. At eleven o'clock she got up

corridor, a long narrow passage from which doors open into rooms.

to go back to her own room, but she stopped at the door and looked back.

' "Tell me, Helen," she said, "have you ever heard anyone whistle in the middle of the night?"

' "Never," I said. "But why?" 5

' "Because during the last few nights, at about three o'clock, I've heard a low, clear whistle. I don't sleep well, and it's wakened me. I don't know where it came from — perhaps the next room, perhaps the garden. I thought I would just ask you if you'd heard it." 10

' "No, I haven't. It must be those terrible gypsies."

' "Maybe it is. And yet if it was in the garden, I wonder why you didn't hear it also."

' "Ah, but I sleep better than you do."

' "Oh, well. It doesn't really matter." She smiled at me, 15 and closed my door. A few moments later I heard her key turning in the lock.'

'Indeed!' said Holmes. 'Did you always lock your doors at night?' 20

'Always.'

'And why?'

'I think I told you the doctor keeps a cheetah and a baboon. We didn't feel safe unless our doors were locked.'

'Ah, yes. Please continue.'

'I couldn't sleep, for it was a stormy night. The wind was 25 howling, and the rain was beating and splashing against the windows. Suddenly, through the noise of the storm, I heard the wild scream of a frightened woman. I knew it was my sister's voice.

'I jumped out of bed, and rushed into the corridor. As I 30 opened my door I seemed to hear a low whistle, like the one my sister had described, and a few moments later I heard a sound like a heavy piece of metal falling. As I ran down the corridor I saw my sister at her door. Her face was white with terror, and her whole body was swaying from side to side. I 35 ran to her and put my arms around her, but at that moment she fell to the floor. She beat the floor like someone who is in terrible pain, and her limbs were shaking. While I was bending over her she suddenly cried out in a voice I shall never forget, "O, my God! Helen! It was the band! The speckled band!"

'I called loudly for my stepfather, and met him hurrying
5   from his room. When he reached my sister she was unconscious, and though he poured some medicine down her throat, and sent for another doctor, she never became conscious again, but died quickly.'

'One moment,' said Holmes, 'are you sure about this
10   whistle and the sound like falling metal? You really heard it?'

'That was what they asked me during the inquiry. I *think* I heard it, and yet, in the noise of the storm, I may have been mistaken.'

'And what did they find out at the inquiry?'
15   'Nothing about the cause of death. There were no marks of violence on her body.'

'What do you really think killed your sister, then?'

'I believe she died of fear and nervous shock. However, I've no idea what frightened her.'
20   'Were there gypsies in the garden at that time?'

'Yes, there are nearly always some there.'

'Ah, and what do you think about her cry about a band — a speckled band?'

'Sometimes I think it was just mad talk, or else she may
25   have meant a band of people — perhaps a band of gypsies.'

Holmes shook his head like a man who is not very satisfied.

'All this is difficult to understand,' he said, 'but please go on with your story.'

'That was two years ago, and until recently my life had
30   been lonelier than ever before. A month ago, however, a dear friend, whom I've known for many years, asked me to marry him. My stepfather has made no objection to the marriage, and our wedding will be in a few weeks' time.

'Two days ago some repairs were started on the outside
35   wall of my bedroom, and so I've had to sleep in the room where my sister died. Last night something happened which frightened me greatly. I was lying in bed, thinking of my sister's awful death, when suddenly I heard the low whistle

she had told me about. I jumped up and lit the lamp, but I
could see nothing unusual in the room. I was too frightened
to go back to bed, and I dressed as soon as it was daylight
and hurried out of the house. I drove to the station and came
straight to see you to ask for your help.'   5

'You've done wisely,' said my friend. 'But have you told
me everything?'

'Yes, everything.'

Holmes plans a visit

There was a long silence, during which Holmes leaned his
chin on his hands and stared at the notes he had written in   10
his book.

'This is a very strange case,' he said, at last. 'If we came to
Stoke Moran today could we examine these rooms without
your stepfather seeing us?'

'Yes, because he's coming to London today for some im-   15
portant business. Probably he'll be away from the house all
day, and so there'll be nothing to disturb you.'

'Excellent. You'll come with me, Watson?'

'Yes, of course.'

'Then we shall both come. And what are you going to do,   20
Miss Stoner?'

'I shall return by the twelve o'clock train, so that I'll be at
home when you arrive.'

'And you'll see us early in the afternoon. I've some matters
to deal with in London first. Will you stay for breakfast?'   25

'No, I must go. I feel much better now since I've told you
my troubles. I shall look forward to seeing you again this
afternoon.'

She picked up her coat and bag, and walked quietly from
the room.   30

'Now, what do you think about it all, Watson?' asked
Sherlock Holmes, leaning back in his chair.

'It seems to me to be a very frightening and terrible affair.'

'What about these night-time whistles, and the very peculiar words of the dying woman?'   35

'I think it's a complete mystery.'

'And so do I. And it's for that reason we're going to Stoke
Moran today. I want to see — '

Suddenly my friend was interrupted. The door of the room
was pushed open violently, and a huge man stood before us.
5 He was so tall that his hat actually touched the top of the
doorway, and he was so broad that he almost touched it on
each side. He had a large, evil face, with eyes like a fierce old
eagle's. He stared at us very angrily.

'Which of you is Holmes?' the giant demanded.
10   'That's my name, sir, but I don't know yours,' said my
companion, quietly.

'I am Dr Grimesby Roylott, of Stoke Moran.'

'Indeed, Doctor,' Holmes said softly. 'Please sit down.'

'I will not. My stepdaughter has been here. I've followed
15 her. What's she been saying to you?'

'It's a bit cold for this time of year,' said Holmes.

'What's she been saying to you?' screamed the old man.

'But I've heard the crops have been doing well,' continued
my friend, calmly.
20   'Ha! You won't tell me, eh?' said our visitor, stepping forward. 'I know you, you devil! I've heard of you before.
You're Holmes the trouble-maker!'

My companion smiled. 'Your conversation is very amus-
ing,' said he. 'When you go out, close the door, for the cold
25 air's blowing in.'

'I'll' go when I'm ready. Don't you dare to make any
trouble for me. I know Miss Stoner's been here — I followed
her. I'm a dangerous man, so be careful!'

And, banging his hand down on the table, which broke
30 under the force, he walked out of the room.

'He doesn't seem to be a very friendly person,' said Holmes,
laughing. 'His visit was exciting, however. And now, Watson,
we shall have breakfast, and afterwards I shall go where I
hope to get some information which may help us to solve
35 this problem.'

A very serious matter

It was nearly one o'clock when Sherlock Holmes returned

to the house. He had a sheet of blue paper on which there were notes and figures.

'I've seen the will of Miss Stoner's mother, that is, of Dr Roylott's wife,' he said. 'The total income at the time of his wife's death was about £750 per year. Each daughter would *5* get £250 per year when she married. Therefore, if both girls married, Dr Roylott would have very little money for himself. My morning's work has been very useful, for it's shown he has very good reasons for not wanting his stepdaughters to get married. Watson, this is a very serious matter so we *10* mustn't delay, especially as the Doctor knows we're interested in his affairs. Now, if you're ready call a taxi and we'll drive to the station. And put a gun in your pocket. That, I think, is all we need.'

We caught a train for Stoke Moran, and there we took a *15* taxi and drove for four or five miles through some lovely country. Holmes sat beside me with his arms folded, his hat pulled down over his eyes, and his chin resting on his chest. He was thinking. Suddenly, however, he looked up, tapped me on the shoulder, and pointed over the green fields. 'Look *20* there,' he said.

In the middle of a wood on a gentle slope we could just see the high roof of a very old house.

We drove up to the front door, paid the driver, and the taxi set off again towards Stoke Moran station. *25*

Miss Stoner hurried out to meet us. 'I've been waiting so eagerly for you,' she said, shaking hands with us. 'We're quite safe now as Dr Roylott has gone to London, and he won't be back before evening.'

'We've had the pleasure of meeting the Doctor,' said *30* Holmes; and in a few words he told her what had happened. Her face turned pale as she listened.

'Oh!' she said. 'He's so cunning that I never know when I'm safe from him. What will he do to me when he returns?'

'You must lock your door tonight. If he's violent, we shall *35* take you away to your aunt, Miss Westphail. Now, we mustn't waste any time, so please take us at once to the rooms we want to examine.'

The house was made of old, grey stone. Some of the windows were broken and covered with wooden boards, and parts of the roof were also broken. We could see where someone had been doing repairs to the outside wall, but no one
5   was working there at the time of our visit. Holmes examined carefully the outsides of the windows.

'This, I suppose, is the window of the room where you used to sleep, and the centre one is of your sister's room, and the next is of Dr Roylott's?'
10   'Yes. And now I'm sleeping in the centre room.'

'Ah, yes, because of the repairs. I think, however, this wall doesn't need any repairs.'

'I agree. I believe the Doctor wanted me to move out of my own room, so he began the repairs.'
15   'Ah! that's possible. Now, the corridor is on the other side of these rooms. There are windows in it, of course?'

'Yes, but only very small ones. They're too narrow for anyone to get through.'

'As you both locked your doors at night, then no one
20   could get to them on that side. Now, please go into your own room, and lock the window shutters*.'

Miss Stoner did so, and Holmes then tried every way to force the shutters open, but he could not. There was just no way to open them from the outside. 'Humm!' said he,
25   scratching his chin, 'no gypsy could get through these shutters when they're locked. Well, let's see if we can find an answer to the problem by looking on the inside.'

The room where she died
We walked through a small doorway into the corridor, and then went immediately to the room where Miss Stoner's
30   sister had died.

It was a very nice little room, with a low ceiling. There was a narrow bed in one corner, and a small table in another, and two chairs. Holmes took one of the chairs into a corner, and sat down. He then began to look around the room very care-
35   fully, so that he did not miss one detail. Next he got down on
shutters, covers for windows to keep out light and thieves.

his knees and crawled quickly backwards and forwards, examining the cracks in the floor. Lastly, he walked over to the bed and stared at it, and at the wall behind it, for a long time. There was a little ventilator* about six feet above the bed. 5

'Very strange!' said Holmes. 'Why should anyone want to put a ventilator there, for it opens into another room? Why didn't they put it where it could let in clean air from the garden?'

'How very stupid! I never noticed that before,' said the 10 lady.

'Now, Miss Stoner, you must let us examine the room which this ventilator opens into.'

Dr Grimesby Roylott's bedroom was larger than his step-daughter's. There was not much furniture; only a bed, a shelf 15 full of books, a plain wooden chair against the wall, a round table, and a large iron safe. Holmes walked slowly round and examined each of them with great interest.

'What's in here?' he asked, tapping the safe.

'The Doctor's business papers, I suppose.' 20

'There isn't a cat in it, for example?'

'No. What a strange idea!'

'Well, look at this!' He picked up a small saucer of milk which was on the top of the safe.

'No, we don't have a cat. But there's a cheetah, and a 25 baboon.'

'Ah, yes, of course! Well, a cheetah is just a big cat; and yet a saucer of milk would scarcely be enough for it.'

He next went to the wooden chair and examined the seat with the greatest attention. 'Ah!' he said, and then stood up. 30 'Ah! it's an evil world, and when a clever man becomes a criminal, it's the worst of all.'

When Holmes had finished his investigations we went into the garden and walked about for a while in silence. Then he said, 'It's absolutely necessary, Miss Stoner, that you should 35 follow my instructions in every detail.'

*ventilator, an opening for letting fresh air into a room.

'I shall certainly do so.'

'The situation is very serious. Your life is in great danger, and therefore you must obey me completely.'

'I'll do whatever you tell me to do.'

5   'Firstly, Dr Watson and I must spend the night in your room.'

Both Miss Stoner and I looked at him in amazement.

'Let me explain. You must stay in your room, pretending to be sick, when your stepfather comes back. Then, when
10 you hear him going to bed, you must open the shutters of your window, and put a lamp there as a signal to us. We'll be waiting at the end of the garden. Then you must go into your own bedroom. I'm sure you can manage there in spite of the repairs.'

15   'Ah, yes, easily. But what will you do?'

'We shall spend the night in your room, and we shall try to find out what causes this noise which has disturbed you.'

'I think, Mr Holmes, you already know what it is,' said Miss Stoner, laying her hand on my companion's sleeve.

20   'Perhaps I do.'

'Then you must tell me the cause of my sister's death.'

'I should prefer to have more proof before I tell you. And now, Miss Stoner, we must leave you before the Doctor returns and sees us. Goodbye, and be brave, for we shall soon
25 destroy the dangers which are frightening you.'

Great danger!

'Do you know, Watson,' said Holmes, as we sat together in the darkness at the end of the garden, 'I'm a little worried about taking you with me tonight. There's a risk of great danger.'

30   'You know I like danger. But evidently you've seen something in those rooms which I didn't notice.'

'You saw the ventilator?'

'Yes, but I don't think it's a very dangerous or even unusual thing to have a ventilator between two rooms. It was
35 so small that a rat could hardly get through it.'

'I knew that we should find a ventilator even before we came to Stoke Moran.'

'My dear Holmes!' I said in surprise.

'Oh, yes, I did. You remember Miss Stoner told us her sister could smell Dr Roylott's cigar. Now that suggests at once that there must be some kind of opening between the two rooms, as Miss Stoner told us also that there are no doors between them.'

'I can't see any connection between that and the crime.'

'Did you notice anything peculiar about the bed?'

'No.'

'It was screwed to the floor so that it couldn't be moved about. Have you ever seen a bed fastened to the floor like that?'

'Holmes,' I cried, 'I'm beginning to understand a little of what you're talking about. We're only just in time to prevent another dreadful crime!'

Then, suddenly, as I was speaking, we saw a bright light shining from the dark house.

'That's the signal,' said Holmes, jumping up. 'It comes from the middle window.'

We went carefully through the trees, but as we were about to step through the window, something leaped out of the bushes beside us. It ran on to the grass with waving limbs, and then went quickly across the garden into the darkness.

'My God!' I whispered, 'did you see it?'

Just for a moment Holmes was as surprised as I was, and his hand held my wrist tightly. Then he started to laugh quietly.

'That was the baboon!' he whispered.

I remembered then that there was a cheetah too; perhaps it might attack us at any moment. I must confess I felt a lot safer when we had got into the room. My companion closed the shutters gently and looked around the room. Then, coming over to me, he said in a very low voice: 'We must sit without a light. He could see it through the ventilator.'

I moved my head to show I had heard him.

'Don't go to sleep; it's too dangerous. Get your gun ready

in case we should need it. I'll sit on the side of the bed, and you sit on that chair.'

I took out my gun and put it on the table.

Holmes had a long thin stick which he had brought from
5 the garden. He put this beside him, and a box of matches. Then he put out the lamp, and we sat quietly in the darkness.

I shall never forget that dreadful night! I could not hear a sound, not even the sound of breathing, and yet I knew my friend was wide awake and sitting only a few feet from me.
10 The shutters kept out the moonlight, and we waited in complete darkness. Sometimes we heard the sound of a nightbird, and once, at the window, we heard a strange animal noise, and we knew that the cheetah was wandering freely in the garden. Time seemed to move·very slowly as we sat wait-
15 ing silently.

A terrible cry

Suddenly there was a gleam of light from the ventilator, but it disappeared again immediately. Someone in the next room had lit a lamp. I heard a gentle sound of movement, and then all was silent once more. All at once there was an-
20 other sound, like steam escaping from a kettle. The moment that we heard it, Holmes leaped away from the bed, lit a match, and started hitting the bed violently with his stick.

'You see it, Watson?' he shouted. 'You see it?'

But I saw nothing. Just then Holmes lit another match,
25 and I heard a low, clear whistle; but the sudden flash of the match blinded me for a second so that I could not see what my friend had been striking at with his stick. I could see, however, that his face was very pale, and it had a look of horror and disgust.
30 He had stopped striking at the bed, and was now staring at the ventilator. Then, suddenly, there was the most terrible cry I have ever heard. It grew louder and louder, a shout of pain and fear and anger, and it ended in one long, dreadful scream. Holmes and I stood looking at one another until this
35 terrible cry had disappeared into the silence of the night.

'What can it mean?' I whispered.

'It means that it's all finished,' Holmes answered. 'Take
your gun, and we shall go into the Doctor's room.'

He lit the lamp, and I followed him down the corridor.
Twice he knocked on the bedroom door, but there was no
reply. Then he opened the door and went in, while I followed   5
with my gun ready in my hand.

What we saw was a dreadful sight. There was a lamp on the
table which sent out a brilliant beam of light on to the iron
safe. The door of the safe was open. Beside this table Dr
Roylott was sitting on the wooden chair. His chin was   10
pointing upwards, and his eyes were fixed in an awful stare
at the corner of the ceiling. Round his head was a peculiar
yellow band, with brown speckles, and it appeared to be
bound tightly to him.

As we entered he neither spoke nor moved.   15

'The band! The speckled band!' whispered Holmes.

I took a step forward. At once the band began to move,
and slowly, from amongst his hair, a head, with the shape of
a diamond, started to rise. It was a dreadful snake.

'It's a swamp adder!' cried Holmes. 'The most dangerous   20
snake in India. He has died within seconds of its bite. Let's
kill this awful creature, and then we can move Miss Stoner to
a safer place, and also tell the police what has happened.'

As Holmes spoke, he hit the snake with his stick and broke
its back. Then he threw it into the iron safe and shut the   25
door.

Holmes explains

Those are the facts concerning the death of Dr Grimesby
Roylott, of Stoke Moran. We took care of the frightened girl
as well as we could, and the next morning we took her to   30
stay with her good aunt. After this we reported the whole
matter to the police, and the next day we returned to London. On the train Sherlock Holmes explained to me the
details of the case which I still did not understand.

'At first,' he said, 'I arrived at the wrong answer. It was   35
the gypsies and the use of the word "band" which caused me
to go wrong. However, when we discovered that the bed was

fastened to the floor, and that there was a small ventilator above it, I had an idea. I thought that something might pass through the ventilator to get on to the bed. Immediately, I thought of a snake, because I knew one of Dr Roylott's friends used to send him animals from India.

'Then I thought of the whistle. Of course, he had to be able to call back the snake. He'd trained it, probably by giving it milk, to return to him when he whistled. He used to put it through the ventilator because he knew it would crawl down the wall to the bed. It might not bite the girl immediately, but if he kept putting it through the ventilator, he knew it would finally bite and kill her.

'When I examined his chair I noticed he had the habit of standing on it, and he would have to stand on it if he wanted to reach the ventilator.

'The noise like metal falling which Miss Stoner heard, was caused by her stepfather quickly closing the door of the safe when he'd put the snake back inside it.

'That other noise, like steam escaping, which we heard, was the sound of the snake; and when I was striking at the bed with my stick, I was trying to kill the snake.'

'Ah, yes,' I said, 'and when you attacked it, it went back through the ventilator.'

'And then it attacked its master. I'm sure it was very angry after it had felt my stick, and so attacked the first person it saw. In this way, I suppose, I'm responsible for Dr Grimesby Roylott's death. However, my dear Watson, I don't think that this'll ever worry me very much.'

The Goblins* and the Grave-digger

In an old English town, a long, long time ago, there was a grave-digger called Gabriel Grub, who worked in the church-yard.* He was a lonely man, and he was always angry. He had only one friend, and that was himself. He looked at every
5 merry face with a scowl* of evil temper, which, of course, frightened the people and stopped them from trying to be friendly with him.

One Christmas Eve, a little before it got dark, Gabriel put his spade on his shoulder, lit his lamp, and set off for
10 the churchyard. He had to finish digging a grave by next morning, and as he was feeling unhappy, he thought if he finished the grave he would feel much better. As he walked through the snow, up the ancient street, he noticed the cheer-ful lights gleaming through the old windows, and heard the
15 loud laughter and merry shouts of the people in the houses. He knew they were busy preparing for the festival the next day. He could see the clouds of steam rising from the pots, and smell the delicious food they were cooking. All this made Gabriel feel even more angry; and when groups of children
20 ran out of the houses, laughing and playing their Christmas games, Gabriel scowled at them. He held the handle of his spade more tightly and walked on thinking of measles, scarlet-fever, and whooping cough, and many other evil diseases which attack little boys and girls.

25 These nasty thoughts made him feel much better, and now he walked along happily. Soon he reached the lane near the churchyard. He had been looking forward to reaching this dark lane, because it was a nice, lonely place, and the people

*goblin, a naughty fairy who likes playing tricks on people.
*churchyard, an area round a church, usually with a wall, which is
    often used as a burial-place.
*scowl, (verb and noun), (to make) a bad-tempered look on the face.

from the town did not like to go there except in daylight, when the sun was shining. Because of this, he was surprised and angry to hear somebody in the lane roaring out a jolly song about a merry Christmas.

As Gabriel walked on, and the voice came nearer, he saw   5
it was a small boy who was singing. The boy was hurrying along to a party in the old street, and he was singing loudly to prepare himself for the party, and also to keep himself from feeling frightened in that lonely lane. So Gabriel waited until the boy came up to him, and then pushed him into a   10
corner, and knocked him on the head with his lamp five or six times, to teach him to be quieter. And as the boy hurried away with his hand to his head, singing quite a different sort of tune, Gabriel Grub laughed happily to himself and entered the churchyard, and locked the gate behind him.   15

He took off his coat, put down his lamp, and got into the unfinished grave. He worked for an hour or so quite cheerfully, even though the earth was hard and it was not easy to break it and lift it out. Although there was a moon, it was a very new one, and so it did not give much light on the   20
grave, which was in the shadow of the church. At any other time this would have made Gabriel angry and miserable, but now he was very happy because he had stopped the boy singing.

A most unusual creature

'Ho! Ho!' laughed Gabriel Grub, as he sat down on his   25
favourite resting-place, which was a flat tombstone.*

'Ho! Ho! Ho!' repeated a voice, just behind him.

Gabriel stopped laughing, and looked round. The churchyard was still and quiet in the pale moonlight. The snow lay hard and smooth upon the ground. Not one faint noise broke   30
the silence of this lonely place. It seemed as if sound itself was frozen.

'It was the echoes,' said Gabriel Grub.

'It was *not*,' said a deep voice.

Gabriel jumped up, and then stood very still with amaze-   35

*tombstone, a stone marking a tomb (grave).

ment and terror; for he saw something which frightened him very, very much.

Close to him there was a most unusual creature sitting on an upright tombstone. His legs, which were extremely long, were crossed under him. His thin arms were bare, and his hands rested on his knees. On his fat, round body he wore a short cloak, all covered with strange coloured designs; and the collar of this cloak was cut into curious points which stood up round his neck. His shoes curled up at his toes into long points also. On his head he had a hat which was wide at the bottom and with a point at the top, and it was decorated with one large feather. This hat was covered with the white snow, and the goblin looked as if he had sat on the same tombstone, very comfortably, for two or three hundred years. He was sitting perfectly still; and he was grinning* at Gabriel Grub with the kind of grin which only a goblin can make.

'It was *not* the echoes,' said the goblin.

Gabriel Grub was so frightened that he could not speak.

'What are you doing here on Christmas Eve?' asked the goblin, sternly.

'I came to dig a grave, sir,' said Gabriel Grub.

'What man wanders among graves and churchyards on such a night as this?' cried the goblin.

'Gabriel Grub! Gabriel Grub!' screamed a whole choir of voices that seemed to fill the churchyard. Gabriel looked round in terror, but he could see nothing.

The goblin put out his tongue at the trembling Grub, and then raising his voice, he said:

'And who, then, is our fair and just prize?'

'Gabriel Grub! Gabriel Grub!' shouted the wild voices again.

The goblin grinned a broader grin than before, as he said, 'Well, what do you say about this?'

The grave-digger tried very hard to speak. 'It's — it's — very curious, sir,' he replied, half dead with fright, 'but I think I'll go back and finish my work, sir, if you don't mind.'

*grin, (verb and noun), (to make) a broad smile.

'Oh, the grave, eh?' said the goblin. 'Who digs graves on Christmas Eve when other men are merry — and who enjoys doing it?'

Again the mysterious voices shouted, 'Gabriel Grub! Gabriel Grub!'

'I'm sorry, but it seems my friends want you, Gabriel,' said the goblin, putting out his tongue again — and a most amazing tongue it was — 'Ah, yes, it seems my friends want you, Gabriel. We know the man with the angry face and the terrible scowl who came down the street tonight, looking at the children with evil in his eyes. We know the man who struck the boy, because he was jealous that the boy could be merry, and he could not. We know him, we know him.'

And then the goblin laughed a loud, high laugh, and threw his legs up in the air and stood on his head, or rather on the point of his tall hat. Then he rolled over and over, right to the grave-digger's feet, and there he sat with his legs crossed under him again.

'I — I — must leave you now, sir,' said the poor grave-digger, making an effort to move.

'Leave us!' cried the goblin. 'Gabriel Grub is going to leave us? Ho! Ho! Ho!'

The goblins' cave

As the goblin laughed, hundreds of goblins rushed into the churchyard, and began jumping over the tombstones, without ever stopping to rest or take a breath.

The game became faster and faster as the goblins leaped faster and faster. They rolled and rolled all over the place, and flew like footballs over the tombstones. The grave-digger's brain was beginning to go round and round ·as he watched the goblins; and then, suddenly, the goblin king jumped towards him, put his hand upon his collar, and sunk with him through the earth.

They went down very fast, and when Gabriel Grub had had time to get back his breath, which had been taken away by the speed of his descent, he found that he was in what appeared to be a large cave. All round him were crowds of

goblins, ugly and stern. Sitting on a raised seat in the middle
of the room was his friend from the churchyard — the goblin
king.

'It's cold tonight,' said the king of the goblins, 'very cold.
Let's have a cup of something warm to drink!'   5

At this command, half a dozen goblins hastily disappeared,
and presently returned with a cup of liquid fire. This they
presented to the king.

'Ah!' cried the goblin, whose cheeks and throat shone as
he swallowed the flame, 'this warms one, indeed! Bring an-   10
other cup for Mr Grub!'

It was useless for the unfortunate grave-digger to refuse it.
One of the goblins held him while another poured the blazing
liquid down his throat. Then the whole crowd of them roared
with laughter as he coughed and choked and wiped away the   15
tears which poured from his eyes after he had swallowed the
burning drink.

'And now,' said the king, 'show to this man of misery and
anger a few of the pictures from our great collection.'

As the goblin king said this, a thick cloud, which hid the   20
far end of the cave, slowly disappeared. Behind it there was
a small room with cheap furniture, but everything was neat
and clean. A group of little children were playing round their
mother's chair. Occasionally the mother rose and moved the
curtains aside, as if to see if someone was coming. At last   25
there was a knock on the door; the mother opened it, and
the children crowded round her and clapped their hands as
their father entered. Then, as he sat down in his favourite
chair, they climbed over his knees, and his wife sat beside
him. All seemed to be happiness and comfort.   30

But then the scene began to change. Now there was a small
bedroom, and in it the youngest and most beautiful child lay
dying. Even as Gabriel watched him with a feeling of interest
which he had never felt before, the child's brothers and sisters
crowded round the little bed and lifted his tiny hand, so cold   35
and heavy. But the touch of his cold hand frightened them,
and in fear, they looked at his little face; for they saw he was
dead.

'What do you think of *that*?' said the goblin, turning his large face towards Gabriel Grub.

Gabriel said something about it being very sad, and he looked a little ashamed as the goblin looked at him with
5   angry eyes.

'*You* miserable man!' said the goblin, and there was the sound of hatred in his voice. 'You — ' he seemed to want to say something else, but anger stopped his words, so he lifted up his long thin legs, and gave Gabriel Grub a good hard kick.
10   Immediately after this all the goblins started kicking him, without any mercy, just to teach him a good hard lesson.

'Show him some more!' said the king of the goblins.

And again the cloud disappeared, and this time there was a beautiful country scene. The sun shone in a clear blue sky,
15   the water gleamed in the sunlight, and the trees looked greener, and the flowers looked prettier, than they do in real life. The streams made a pleasant sound; the branches moved gently in the light wind which whispered amongst the leaves; and the birds sang in the trees. The tiniest leaf, the smallest
20   blade of grass, was filled with life. The ant came out to do her daily work; the butterfly* danced in the warm sunlight; millions of insects spread their shining wings; and Man walked about, delighted with the beauty of the scene.

'You *are* a miserable man!' said the king of the goblins, in
25   an even greater rage than before. And again he kicked the grave-digger, and again the goblins followed the example of their chief.

Gabriel learns at last

Many times the cloud went and came, and many lessons it taught to Gabriel Grub, who, although his back was very
30   sore from the goblins' kicks, watched every scene with interest. He saw that men who worked hard were cheerful and happy; and he saw that even for people who had no education, the beauty of nature was a never-ending joy. He saw that men like himself, who scowled at the cheerfulness of
35   others, were the most evil creatures in the world. And most
butterfly, insect with large coloured wings.

important of all, when he compared all the good in the world
with all the evil, he suddenly realized that it was a very
pleasant world after all.

As soon as he had realized this, the cloud which had just
covered the last picture, now began to spread around him.   *5*
One by one, the goblins faded from his sight; and as the last
one disappeared, he fell asleep.

The day had dawned when Gabriel Grub awoke, and he
found that he was lying on the flat tombstone in the churchyard. His coat, spade, and lamp were scattered on the ground,   *10*
and were all white with new snow. The stone on which he
had first seen the goblin stood upright before him, and the
grave which he had been digging the night before was not far
away. At first he began to wonder if his adventures had really
happened, but he felt a great pain in his back when he tried   *15*
to stand up, and then he knew he had indeed been kicked by
the goblins. So he stood up as well as he could, and after he
had brushed the snow off his coat, he put it on, and moved
off towards the town.

What happened to the grave-digger?

But he had changed, and he could not bear to think of   *20*
returning to a place where no one would either believe his
story, or believe that he had changed. He hesitated for a few
seconds, and then set off to look for some other place where
men would welcome him, and children would not run away
from him in fear.   *25*

The lamp and the spade were found that day in the churchyard. At first everyone had their own opinion about what
had happened to the grave-digger, but soon they all decided
that he had been carried away by the goblins. Some people
even said they had seen him flying through the air on a black   *30*
horse, which was blind in one eye, and had the claws of a
lion and the tail of a bear. After a while this story was generally believed. In fact, after a few years, the people began to
think the story was actual history, and that is the way they
think of it even today.   *35*

The Island of Voices

Keola was the husband of Lehua, daughter of Kalamake, the wise man of Molokai, and he lived with the father of his wife. No man was more cunning than Kalamake; he could read men's fortunes in the stars; he could tell what would happen
5 in the future by the bodies of the dead; and he could go alone into the highest parts of the mountains, into the region of the evil goblins.

For this reason, the people thought that Kalamake was the greatest fortune-teller* in the whole kingdom of Hawaii.
10 They would buy and sell, or get married, according to his advice. But also, the people feared him more than they feared any other man, because some of his enemies got sick and died, and others just disappeared. It was said he had the art or the skills of the old heroes*. Men had seen him at night
15 stepping from one cliff to another; they had seen him walking in the high forest, and his head and shoulders were above the trees.

This Kalamake was a strange looking man. He was one of the island people, and yet he was whiter than any foreigner.
20 His hair was the colour of dry grass, and his eyes were red and very fierce.

There was one thing about his wife's father which puzzled Keola; and this was the fact that Kalamake always had plenty of money to pay for what he bought, whether to eat or to
25 drink, or to wear; and he paid for everything in bright new dollars. Yet he never sold anything, nor planted crops, nor worked for wages, and no one knew where he obtained so many silver coins.

It happened one day that Keola's wife went on a visit to

*fortune-teller, a person who can tell what will happen in the future.
*hero, a man who is respected for bravery or other noble qualities.

the other side of the island, and the men went out fishing. But Keola was an idle person, and he lay in front of his house and watched the waves breaking on the beach, and the birds flying about the cliff. As usual, he was thinking of the bright silver dollars. When he lay in bed he would wonder why there were so many, and when he woke in the mornings, he would wonder why they were all new. But on this day he felt he would find an answer, for he thought he had discovered the place where Kalamake kept his treasure, which was a locked desk by the kitchen wall. Just the night before, he had found a way to look into it, and he saw a big empty bag lying there. And this was the day when the steamship came; he could see its smoke out over the sea. It would soon arrive with a month's goods, tins of strange fish, and cheese, and all kinds of rare luxuries for Kalamake.

A secret matter

'Now, if he can pay for his goods today,' Keola thought, 'I shall know for certain that the man is a magician*, and that the dollars come out of the Devil's pocket, because the bag is empty.' While he was thinking this, Kalamake came up behind him, looking angry.

'Is that the ship?' he asked.

'Yes,' said Keola. 'It will soon be here.'

'Then I must tell you a secret matter, Keola. Come into the house.'

Kalamake made Keola close the shutters of the windows, while he himself locked all the doors. Then he opened the desk, and from it he took a pair of shell necklaces, a bundle of dry leaves, and a green branch of palm*. Then he took out a mat, which had been made with great skill and care. Next, he put the leaves in a tin pan. After this, he and Keola put on the necklaces, and stood upon the opposite corners of the mat.

'It is time to begin,' said the magician. 'Do not be afraid.'

He put a flame to the leaves, and began to mutter and wave

*magician, a person who has the skill to do magic.
*palm, a sort of tree which grows in warm climates, and which has large
    wide leaves.

Margin line numbers: 5, 10, 15, 20, 25, 30

the branch of palm. At first the light was dim because the shutters were closed. But the leaves began to burn, and soon the room glowed with the burning. The flames danced about Keola, and the rising smoke made his head feel strange, and
5   his eyes became dark, and the sound of Kalamake muttering rang through his ears. Then, suddenly, the mat they were standing on began to move. In a second the room was gone, and all the breath had gone out of Keola's body. The sun shone upon his eyes and head, and he saw he was on a beach,
10   with the great waves roaring. He and Keola were standing there on the same mat, unable to speak, choking, and trying to hold on to one another, and rubbing their eyes with their hands.

The magic beach

'What was that?' cried Keola, who recovered first, because
15   he was younger. 'It was like death. And where are we?'
'That is not important,' said Kalamake. 'While I am re-covering, go to the edge of the wood and bring me leaves of the plants and trees there — three small bundles of each. And be quick. We must be home again before the ship comes.'
20   And he sat on the sand to get his breath back.
Keola walked across the shining sand, which had many curious shells lying in it.
'Where is this strange beach?' he thought. 'This is not like Hawaii. I will come here again and gather shells.'
25   Then, as Keola went towards the trees, he saw a young woman who was wearing nothing except a skirt of leaves. She stood looking towards the beach, but it seemed she did not see him.
'Hello,' he said. 'Do not be afraid. I will not harm you.'
30   But he had scarcely begun to speak before the young woman ran away into the wood.
'That is very strange behaviour,' thought Keola, and with-out thinking about what he was doing, he ran after her.
As she ran, the girl kept shouting in a language that they
35   do not speak in Hawaii, but Keola understood some of the words, and he knew she was calling out to warn others. And

presently he saw some people running — men, women and children, all running and crying in fear. And he began to feel afraid himself, and returned to Kalamake. He gave him the leaves, and told him what had happened.

5   'You must take no notice of such things,' said the magician. 'All this is like a dream, and it will disappear and you will forget it.'

'It seemed no one saw me,' said Keola.

'And no one did,' Kalamake replied. 'They cannot see us, 10 but they can hear us, and so you must speak softly, as I do.'

Then he made a circle of stones round the mat, and in the middle of it he put the leaves.

'It will be your duty,' he said, 'to keep the leaves burning. They will only burn for a short time, and while they are 15 burning I must do my business. And before the ashes turn black, the same power which brought us here will bring us home again. Get a match ready; and call me before all the leaves have burnt away, or else I will be left here.'

As soon as the leaves were flaming, the magician leaped 20 like a deer out of the circle, and began to run along the beach. While he ran he also picked up shells; and it seemed to Keola that they glittered as he took them. The leaves burnt quickly with a clear flame, and soon Keola only had a few left. Kalamake was far away, running and gathering shells.

25   'Back!' cried Keola. 'Back! The leaves are nearly gone!' Kalamake turned, and ran fast, but the leaves burned faster. The flame was ready to go out when, with a great leap, he jumped onto the mat. The flame went out, and suddenly the beach, the sun and the sky were all gone, and they were 30 standing in the dim room again. Between them on the mat there was a pile of shining dollars. Keola ran to open the shutters, and then he saw the steamship close to the beach.

The same night Kalamake came to Keola and put five dollars in his hand.

35   'Keola,' he said, 'if you are a wise man, you will think you slept and dreamed this afternoon in front of the house. I know how to keep secrets, and I use people who have bad memories to help me.'

Although Kalamake did not refer again to that affair, it stayed in Keola's memory. He had been lazy before, but now he did nothing at all.

'Why should I work,' he thought, 'when my wife's father makes dollars from sea-shells?' 5

He bought fine clothes, and soon he had spent all his money. But he was not satisfied, and he said to himself, 'I should have bought a concertina*, and then I would have been happy all day playing it.' And then he began to feel angry with Kalamake. 10

'This man has the soul of a dog,' he thought. 'He can gather dollars on the beach at any time, but he leaves me without a concertina! He should be careful because I am not stupid. I am as cunning as he is, and I know his secret.' Then he spoke to his wife Lehua, and complained to her that her 15 father had treated him badly.

'Do not complain about my father, Keola,' she replied, 'for he is a dangerous and powerful man. If you annoy him, he will hold you between his thumb and finger and eat you like a peanut.' 20

Now Keola was really afraid of Kalamake, but he was angry. He went outside immediately to where the magician was sitting.

'Kalamake,' he said, 'I want a concertina.'

'Do you, indeed?' said Kalamake. 25

'Yes,' he said, 'and I shall have it. A man who picks up dollars on the beach can certainly afford a concertina.'

'I did not know you were so brave,' replied the magician. 'I thought you were a nervous, useless person, and I cannot describe how happy I am to find that I was wrong. A con- 30 certina? You shall have the best. And tonight, as soon as it is dark, you and I shall go to find the money.'

'Shall we return to the beach?' asked Keola.

'No, no!' cried Kalamake. 'You must begin to learn more of my secrets. Last time I taught you to pick up shells; this 35 time I shall teach you to catch fish.'

*concertina, a musical wind-instrument with keys at each end.

The Sea of the Dead

As soon as it was dark, Kalamake and Keola set off in a small boat. There were big waves, and a strong wind blew from the west. The magician had a lamp which he lit, and the two men sat and smoked cigars. They talked about magic,
5 and about all the money they would get. And Kalamake talked like a father.

Presently he looked all around and above him at the stars, and back at the island, and he seemed to be thinking about where they were.

10 'Look!' he cried, 'there is Molokai already far behind us, and by these three stars I know I have come to the right place. This part of the sea is called the Sea of the Dead. It is very deep, and the bottom of the sea is all covered with the bones of men. The flow of the sea is to the north, and it
15 moves faster than a shark can swim. Any man who falls from a ship here, goes down, and his bones lie on the bottom with the others, and the gods take his spirit.'

Keola felt frightened when he heard these words. And by the light of the stars and the lamp, he could see the magician
20 was changing. His head grew as large as a barrel; and still he grew and grew, just as a cloud grows on a mountain. Keola sat and shook with fear, and the boat rushed across the great waves.

'And now,' said the magician, 'what do you think about
25 that concertina? Are you sure you would not like something else? Oh, how sad, but I see you are feeling sick. And now I think I should get out of this small boat, for my body is getting very large. If we are not careful, the boat will sink.'

He put his huge legs over the side, and stood in the deep
30 sea. His head and shoulders rose like a high island from the water, and the waves beat and broke upon his chest as if it were a cliff. The boat still rushed towards the north, but he reached out his finger and thumb and broke the side like a biscuit, and Keola fell into the sea. And Kalamake crushed
35 the pieces of the boat in his hand, and threw them miles away into the darkness.

'Excuse me for taking the lamp,' said he, 'but I have a long way to walk. The land is far, and the bottom of the sea is rough, and I feel the bones under my toes.'

And he turned and went off walking through the sea; and he held the lamp high over his head, and the waves broke white about him as he went.

There was never a man more frightened than Keola. Indeed he swam, but he swam like a puppy which has been thrown into the water to drown. He could think of nothing but Kalamake's huge swelling face, which was as big as a mountain, and his shoulders, which were as broad as an island. He thought too of the concertina, and he felt ashamed. Then he thought of the dead men's bones, and he shook with fear.

Rescue

Suddenly he saw a dark shape against the stars, and he heard the voices of men. He cried out aloud. A voice answered; and above him he saw a ship rising on the great waves. He caught a rope with his two hands. The next second he was buried in the rushing waves, but immediately he was pulled on board by the sailors.

They gave him a drink and biscuits, and dry clothes, and told him they were going to trade among the islands. They said one of the sailors had fallen off the ship during a storm, and Keola could have his job.

In some ways the ship was a good place. There was plenty of good food every day, and the captain was a fine man. However, the mate was the most difficult person to please that Keola had ever met. This mate beat and cursed him daily, both for the things he did and for the things he did not do. Keola suffered much pain from these beatings, because the mate was very strong; and so he decided to run away.

They had sailed for about a month when they came near an island. It was a clear night, the sea was calm, and they could see the palm trees along the edge of the beach. The captain and mate looked at it through a telescope and talked about it when they were standing beside Keola, who was steering the ship. They told Keola to steer away from the island because there were dangerous rocks along its coast.

But when the captain and mate went away, Keola thought:

'This island would be a good place for me. If no ships go there, then the mate will never come, and it is not possible that Kalamake can get this far.'

So he kept steering the ship nearer the shore. He had to do this quietly, but he managed it. Presently the land was close, and the sound of the waves hitting the beach was loud. Just then the mate came back.

'What are you doing?' he roared. 'Do you want to put the ship on the rocks?'

And he rushed at Keola, but Keola jumped right over the side of the ship and into the smooth sea. When he came up again, he saw the mate steering the ship away from the island, and he could hear him cursing. The sea was warm, and Keola had his sailor's knife, so he was not afraid of sharks. A short distance in front of him there was a break in the line of the land like the entrance of a harbour. The tide was flowing strongly, and it took him through quickly. He floated there in the shallow water, bright with ten thousand stars, and all around him was the land, with its line of palm trees. And he was amazed, because he had never seen an island like this before.

The Island of Voices

The time Keola spent on the island was divided into two periods — the period when he was alone, and the period when he was with the tribe.

At first he searched everywhere and found no men, but only some huts and the marks of fires. But the ashes of the fires were cold and the rain had washed them away; and the wind had blown down some of the huts. It was here he made his home. He made a hook from a piece of shell, and fished and cooked his fish. He gathered green coconuts and drank their juice, for there was no water on the island. The days passed slowly for Keola. At night he lay in his hut and trembled with fear. Many times he thought it would be better if his bones were rolling with the others on the bottom of the sea.

During all this time he stayed on one side of the island, for the huts were there, and the palms grew best there too. He only went once to the other side of the island. He looked only once at the beach there, and what he saw frightened him greatly. The look of it, with its bright sand and strange shells   *5* reminded him of some place.

'It cannot be,' he thought, 'and yet it is very like the beach where Kalamake gathers his dollars.'

So after that he stayed away from that side.

About a month later, the people of the island returned in   *10* six large boats. They were fine people, and they spoke a language which sounded very different from the language of Hawaii, but so many of the words were the same that Keola could understand it. They were kind to Keola, and built him a house, and gave him a wife. But it surprised him that they   *15* never sent him to work with the young men.

It alarmed him to find that his wife was the same girl who had run away from him in the wood. He was certain then that, although he had sailed such a long way, the place where he had come to was indeed where the magician gathered his   *20* dollars, and the place where he walked invisible. So Keola stayed away from the beach of shells on the other side of the island, and stayed as much as he could in his little hut.

He asked the people of the tribe many questions, and learned much from them. The island was called the Island of   *25* Voices. It belonged to the tribe, but they also lived on another island, three hours' sail to the south. Once a year they came to the Island of Voices to fish. They gave this name to the island because on one side of it many invisible devils lived. Day and night you could hear them talking in strange   *30* languages; and day and night little fires blazed up, but they disappeared again in a moment. They told him also that these fires were only on that side, but that the devils there were very fierce and powerful. Unfortunately the tribe had often to go there to gather wood for their fires. Then, with roars of   *35* anger, the devils would chase them away. Once a chief had thrown a spear at one of the voices, and the same night he fell off a coconut palm and was killed.

In spite of these stories, Keola began to feel quite safe after a while. He began to enjoy his life. He was kind to his wife, and the girl began to love him very much. One day he came to the hut and found her on the ground crying.

5   'What is matter with you?' asked Keola.

She said it was nothing.

The same night she woke him. The lamp burned very softly, but he could still see that she was very unhappy.

'Keola,' she said, 'put your ear to my mouth so that I may
10   whisper, for no one must hear us. Today, before the boats are ready to leave again, you must go to the other side of the island, and lie in the wood. You and I shall choose the place soon, and hide some food there. Every night I shall come near this place and sing. When a night comes and you do not
15   hear me, you shall know we have left the island, and you may come home again in safety.'

Keola was amazed.

'What do you mean?' he cried. 'I cannot live among the devils. I will not stay behind on this island. I want to leave it.'
20   'You will never leave it alive, my poor Keola,' said the girl. 'I will tell you the truth. My people are eaters of men; but this they keep secret. Why do you think they did not ask you to work? It is to keep you fat, my poor husband.'

Keola was very afraid. He had heard stories of man-eaters
25   in the islands, and these had always frightened him.

'Will I never be safe?' he cried, jumping up. 'It seems whatever I do I will die. But if I must die, let me die the quickest way. Since I must be eaten, let me be eaten by devils and not by men. Goodbye.'
30   And he left her there, and walked to the other side of the island.

Keola among the Devils

There was nobody on the beach, but all around him the voices talked and whispered, and the little fires blazed up and then went out. He saw the shells disappear all about him,
35   but he could see no one pick them up.

'It is clear Kalamake is not here,' he thought, 'or he would have attacked me.'

He sat down at the edge of the wood, for he was tired, and put his chin on his hands. The magic on the beach continued. There were voices, and fires blazing and then dying, and the shells disappeared and were replaced even while he looked. It made his head feel strange when he thought of the millions of dollars lying there on the beach. But he continued to sit there, and wait for the tribe or the devils to come for him. After a long time, he fell asleep, and then he forgot the island and all his terrors.

Early the next morning, before the sun was up, a rushing sound woke him. He awoke in fear, for he thought the tribe had caught him; but it was not that. On the beach in front of him the voices called and shouted angrily to one another, and it seemed they were all rushing past him.

'What is this?' Keola said to himself. 'It is not me they are angry at, for they have run past me. I shall see what all the trouble is about.' So he forgot about his fear and started running with the voices.

He reached one point of the island, and from this he could see the next point. Coming from that direction he could hear the terrible cries of men, and as he got nearer he could also hear the sound of trees being cut down. Then he knew that the men of the tribe were cutting down the devils' magic trees, and the voices had come to stop them. He kept on running with the voices because he wanted to see what would happen. He crossed the beach, and came to the edge of the wood.

He stood there amazed. One tree had fallen and others were partly cut. There were the men of the tribe fighting wildly with an enemy they could not see. There were many wounded men, and some lay dead on the ground.

Have you ever seen a boy with a toy sword, leaping and cutting the empty air, as he fights his imaginary enemy? Well that was how the man-eaters were fighting, except that their enemies were not imaginary — they were invisible. They could see the weapons, but they could not see the hands which held them.

For a while Keola watched this amazing fight as though he was dreaming; and then the chief of the tribe saw him and
5 called out his name. The whole tribe saw him then, and their eyes flashed with hatred.

Keola goes home

'I have stood here too long,' thought Keola, and he ran out of the wood and down the beach, not knowing where he would find safety.
10 'Keola!' said a voice beside him on the empty sand.

'Lehua! is that you?' he cried, and looked around for her, but could see no one.

'I saw you pass before,' the voice answered, 'but you did not hear me. Quick! Get the magic leaves, and let us get away
15 from this place.'

'You are there with the mat?' he asked.

'Here, at your side,' said she; and he felt her arms round him. 'Quick! Get the leaves before my father can get back.'

So Keola ran as fast as he could and fetched the leaves.
20 Lehua guided him back, and put his feet upon the mat, and made the fire. And while it burned, the sound of the battle came out of the wood. Keola stood upon the mat and lis-tened, and watched how Lehua's invisible hands poured leaves onto the fire. She poured them fast, and the flame
25 burned high, and by blowing the fire she made it burn faster. The last leaf burned away, the flame fell, and the shock fol-lowed, and Keola and Lehua found themselves in their room at home in Molokai.

Now that Keola could see his wife, he knew he was safe
30 from the man-eaters and from the devils on the Island of Voices. But there was a another matter, and Lehua and Keola talked about it all night, for they were worried. Kalamake was left behind on the island. If, by the blessing of God, he was trapped there, they would be quite safe. But,
35 if he escaped and returned to Molokai, he would surely destroy his daughter and her husband. They spoke of his

power to swell and grow huge, and they wondered if he could walk the great distance to Molokai through the sea. Keola now knew where the island was, so he fetched his atlas and looked at the distance upon the map. It seemed a long way for the old magician to walk. Still, to help them feel safer, *5* they decided to ask the foreign missionary* for some advice.

So Keola told everything to the missionary who arrived on the next ship. And the missionary was very angry with him for marrying another woman on the Island of Voices.

'However,' he said, 'if you think the old man's money is *10* evil, my advice to you is to give it to the missionary society to help the missionaries to do good work. And also, I think you should keep your extraordinary story secret.'

Keola and Lehua took his advice, and gave a great many dollars to the missionary society. And it seems as though it *15* was very good advice, for since that day Kalamake has never been seen again. But whether he was killed in the battle in the wood, or whether he is still a prisoner on the Island of Voices, who can say?

---

*missionary, a person sent to another country to preach his religion.

The Nightingale* and the Rose

'She said that she would dance with me if I brought her red roses,' cried the young Student, 'but there is no red rose in all my garden.'

From her nest in the oak-tree the Nightingale heard him,
5   and she looked out through the leaves and wondered.

'No red rose in all my garden!' he cried, and his beautiful eyes filled with tears. 'Ah, happiness depends on such little things! I have read all that the wise men have written, and all the secrets of philosophy* are mine, and yet I am unhappy
10 because I have no red rose.'

'Here is a true lover,' said the Nightingale. 'His hair is as dark as the night, and his lips are as red as the rose he desires, but passion* and sorrow have made his face so pale.'

'The Prince is giving a ball tomorrow night,' said the young
15 Student, 'and my love will be there. If I bring her a red rose she will dance with me till dawn. If I bring her a red rose, I shall hold her in my arms, and she will lean her head upon my shoulder and I will hold her hand in mine. But there is no rose in my garden, so I will sit all alone at the ball, and she
20 will pass me by. She will dance only with others, and my heart will break.'

'Night after night I have sung of love,' thought the Nightingale, 'and this gives great joy to me; and yet what is joy to me is pain and suffering to him. Surely love is a
25 wonderful thing. It is more precious and more beautiful than the finest jewels. And the finest jewels cannot buy it, nor is it for sale in the market-place. It may not be bought from the merchants, nor can it be weighed and exchanged for gold.'

'The musicians will play their instruments,' said the young

*nightingale, a small bird which sings sweetly at night as well as during the day.
*philosophy, the search for knowledge, especially knowledge of life.
*passion, strong feelings.

Student, 'and my love will dance to the sound of their music. She will dance so lightly that her feet will not touch the floor, and all will gather round to admire her. But with me she will not dance, for I have no red rose to give her.' And he dropped down on the grass, and covered his face with his hands, and cried.

'Why is he weeping?' said a little Green Lizard*, as he ran past him with his tail in the air.

'Why, indeed?' said a Butterfly, as he flew among the flowers.

'He is weeping for a red rose,' said the Nightingale.

'For a red rose?' they cried. 'How very foolish!'

But the Nightingale knew the secret of the Student's sorrow, and she sat silent in the oak-tree, and thought about the mystery of love.

Suddenly she spread her brown wings and flew away. She passed out of the tree like a shadow and like a shadow she flew across the garden.

In the very centre of the garden there was a beautiful Rose-tree, and when she saw it she flew over to it.

'Give me a red rose,' she cried, 'and I will sing you my sweetest song.'

But the Tree shook its head.

'My roses are white,' it answered, 'as white as the top of a wave, and whiter than the snow upon the mountain. But go to my brother who grows beneath the Student's window, and perhaps he will give you what you want.'

So the Nightingale flew over to the Rose-tree that was growing beneath the Student's window.

'Give me a red rose,' she cried, 'and I will sing you my sweetest song.'

But the Tree shook its head.

'My roses are red,' it answered, 'as red as the feet of the dove*, and redder than the coral* that wave and wave in the ocean-cave. But the frost of winter has frozen my veins, and

*lizard, a four-legged and long-tailed reptile.
*dove, a kind of small bird.
*coral, a hard rock-like substance built on the bottom of the sea by tiny sea-creatures.

bitten with its cold teeth into my buds, and the storm has broken my branches, and I shall have no roses at all this year.'

'One red rose is all I want,' cried the Nightingale, 'only one red rose! Is there no way by which I can get it?'

5 'There is a way,' answered the Tree; 'but it is so terrible that I dare not tell it to you.'

'Tell it to me,' said the Nightingale. 'I am not afraid.'

'If you want a red rose,' said the Tree, 'you must build it out of music sung in the moonlight, and stain it with your 10 own heart's blood. You must sing to me with your breast* against a thorn*. All night long you must sing to me, and the thorn must go through your heart, and your life-blood must flow into my veins, and become mine.'

'Death is a great price to pay for a red rose,' cried the Nightingale, 'and Life is very dear to everyone. Yet Love is 15 better than Life, and surely the heart of a bird is not so precious as the heart of a man?'

Love is better than Life

So she spread her brown wings and flew away. She moved across the garden like a shadow, and like a shadow she flew into the tree.

20 The young Student was still lying on the grass, and the tears were not yet dry in his beautiful eyes.

'Be happy,' cried the Nightingale, 'be happy, you shall have your red rose. I will build it out of music sung by moonlight, and stain it with my own heart's blood. All I ask you 25 in return is that you will be a true lover, for Love is wiser than Philosophy, though he is wise, and Love is stronger than Power, though he is strong. Love's wings are the colour of flame, and flame-coloured is his body, and his lips are as sweet as honey.'

30 The Student looked up from the grass, and listened, but he could not understand what the Nightingale was saying to him, for he only knew the things that are written down in books.

*breast, the upper front part of the bodies of humans and animals.
*thorn, sharp-pointed growth on the stem of a plant.

But the oak-tree understood, and felt sad, for he was very fond of the little Nightingale who had built her nest in his branches.

'Sing me one last song,' he whispered, 'I shall be lonely when you are gone.'   5

So the Nightingale sang to the oak-tree, and her voice was like water bubbling from a silver jar.

When she had finished her song, the Student got up, and pulled a notebook and a pencil out of his pocket.

'The Nightingale sings beautifully,' he said to himself, as   10
he walked through the garden, 'but has she got feelings? I am afraid she has not. In fact she is like most artists; she performs very well, but she is not really sincere. She would not sacrifice herself for others. She thinks only of music. Still, I must admit she can sing very beautifully. What a pity her   15
songs do not mean anything, or do any practical good!' And he went into his room, and lay down on his little wooden bed, and began to think of his love; and, after a time, he fell asleep.

And when the moon shone in the dark sky, the Nightingale   20
flew to the Rose-tree, and put her breast against the thorn. All night long she sang, with her breast against the thorn, and the cold clear moon leaned down and listened. All night long she sang, and the thorn went deeper and deeper into her breast, and her life-blood flowed out of her.   25

She sang first of the birth of love in the heart of a boy and a girl. And on the very top branch of the Rose-tree a magnificent rose began to blossom. The rose grew larger with every song she sang. At first it was pale, like the mist which hangs above the river — but the Tree cried to the Nightingale to   30
press closer against the thorn. 'Press closer, little Nightingale,' cried the Tree, 'or the Day will come before the rose is finished.'

So the Nightingale pressed closer against the thorn, and louder and louder grew her song, for she sang of the birth of   35
passion in the soul of a man and a woman.

And slowly the pale rose changed to a soft pink. But the thorn had not yet reached her heart, so the heart of the rose

remained white, for only the heart's blood of a Nightingale
can make the heart of a rose turn red.

And the Tree cried to the Nightingale to press closer
against the thorn. 'Press closer, little Nightingale,' cried the
Tree, 'or the Day will come before the rose is finished.'   *5*

So the Nightingale pressed closer against the thorn, and the
thorn touched her heart, and a fierce pain went through her.
Terrible, terrible was the pain, and wilder and wilder grew her
song, for she sang of the Love that is made perfect by Death,
which is the Love that does not die in the grave.   *10*

And the magnificent rose turned red, as red as the sky at
dawn.

But the Nightingale's voice grew fainter, and her little
wings began to beat, and her eyes grew dim. Fainter, and
fainter, and fainter grew her song, and she felt something   *15*
choking her in her throat.

Then she sang one last long note of music. The red rose
heard it, and trembled all over with joy, and it opened itself
to the cold morning air.

'Look, look!' cried the Tree, 'the rose is finished now.' But   *20*
the Nightingale did not answer, for she was lying dead in the
long grass, with the thorn in her heart.

Jewels cost more than flowers

And at noon the Student opened his window and looked   *25*
out.

'Why, what a wonderful piece of luck!' he cried. 'Here is a
red rose! I have never seen any rose like it in my life. It is so
beautiful that I am sure it has a long Latin name*,' and he
leaned down and picked it from the branch.   *30*

Then he put on his hat, and ran up to the Professor's house
with the rose in his hand.

The Professor's daughter was sitting in the doorway wind-
ing blue silk, and her little dog was lying at her feet.

'You said that you would dance with me if I brought you   *35*
a red rose,' cried the Student. 'Here is the reddest rose in all

---

*Latin name, most plants have a special scientific name, which is always
in Latin.

the world. You will wear it tonight next to your heart, and as
we dance it will tell you how I love you.'

But the girl only frowned.

'I am afraid it will not look good on my dress,' she an-
5   swered, 'and besides, the nephew of the Prince's Chief Minister has sent me some real jewels, and everybody knows that
jewels cost more than flowers.'

'Well,' said the Student, 'you are ungrateful!' and angrily
he threw the rose into the street, where it fell into the gutter,
10   and an iron wheel went over it.

'Ungrateful!' said the girl. 'I'll tell you something, you are
very rude. And what are you, indeed? Only a Student! Why, I
don't believe you have silver straps on your shoes like the
Minister's nephew has!' And she got up from her chair and
15   went into the house.

'What a silly thing Love is!' said the Student as he walked
away. 'It is not half as useful as Philosophy, for it does not
prove anything, and it is always telling us things which are
not going to happen, and making us believe things which are
20   not true. In fact, Love has no practical use, and nowadays, if
something has no practical use, we should not bother with it.
I shall return to studying Philosophy.'

So he went back to his room and pulled out a great dusty
book, and began to read.

Questions

The Gifts

1. Why did Della not have enough money to buy a present for Jim?
2. Della had two good reasons for crying. What were they?
3. Why do you think Della liked the watch chain?
4. Why did Della feel worried after she had sold her hair and bought the present?
5. What made Jim act so strangely when he got home?
6. Why did Jim say they should put their gifts away for a while?

The Country of The Blind

1. Tell how Nunez got to the Country of the Blind.
2. Name three things which Nunez saw in the valley which made him think the people there were blind.
3. 'The good man who did that must have been as blind as a bat.' What is Nunez talking about in this sentence? Are bats blind? Explain this sentence in your own words.
4. Give two reasons why the blind people thought Nunez was like a child.
5. Why did Nunez think he would be the king of the blind people?
6. Why did he not become their king?
7. Give five reasons why the blind people could move about the valley with confidence.
8. Explain why the people did not want Medina to marry Nunez.
9. How was the old doctor going to 'cure' Nunez of his 'illness'?
10. When Nunez looked at the mountains on the day he was to be made blind, he felt that Medina had become small and far away. Why did he feel this about her?

The Two Friends

1. Why were there no small birds in Paris?
2. Explain why Morissot and Sauvage did not need to talk much when they were fishing.
3. Why were the two friends so unhappy when they met on the street?
4. Why did the French officer tell the two friends the password?
5. What did the two friends think about war? Do you agree with them, or what are your feelings about war?
6. Why do you think the Prussian officer wanted the password?
7. Explain why the Prussians shot the two friends.
8. Do you think Morissot and Sauvage were right not to tell the Prussians the password? Give reasons.

The Bear-Hunt

1. Why did Tolstoy and Demyan decide to follow the bear?
2. Explain why they made a circle round the bear.
3. What did the bear do which shows he was a clever animal?
4. Why did the bear stop attacking Tolstoy?
5. Using information from the story, explain why bear-hunting is a cruel sport.
6. Do you think Tolstoy was right to stop hunting because he believed it was a cruel sport? What do you feel about hunting wild animals?

The Paradise of Thieves

1. Why did Muscari like the restaurant at the hotel so much?
2. What were Ezza's reasons for dressing like an Englishman?
3. How do we know Muscari was not interested in money?
4. Why did Muscari decide to cross the mountains? What did (i) the courier, (ii) the banker, (iii) Ethel think about crossing them?
5. Why do you think Mr Harrogate jumped out of the coach? And why was no one hurt when the coach rolled off the road?

6. What were the brigand chief's plans?

7. What is the answer to Father Brown's question: 'Now, why have we fallen here?'

8. 'Father Brown was correct when he said that the Paradise of Thieves was more like a theatre or stage than a stronghold.' Do you think this statement is true, or false? Give reasons.

9. Mr Harrogate wanted to be captured by the men who were pretending to be brigands. Why did he?

10. Why did Ezza decide to leave Italy?

'Blow Up with The Ship!'

1. How does the haunting of any man begin, according to Wilkie Collins?

2. Why was the *Good Intent* 'a strange name for a ship carrying gunpowder'?

3. Why were there regulations on the ship against smoking, and lighting lamps?

4. What were the sailors' reasons for not liking the pilot?

5. What do you think might have happened to the mate if he had *not* had a fight with the pilot?

6. Give three reasons why the mate thought he would not be rescued.

7. Tell what the mate was doing and thinking when he was lying in the bottom of the ship.

8. What made him go mad?

The Speckled Band

1. What did Miss Stoner ask Sherlock Holmes to do? What did Dr Roylott tell him not to do?

2. How did Julia Stoner die?

3. Why did Dr Roylott not want his stepdaughters to get married?

4. Why did the doctor have repairs done to the wall of Miss Stoner's bedroom?

5. Holmes came to the wrong answers at first. What were these?

6. Why was Miss Stoner's bed fixed to the floor?

7. What was the whistle that Julia heard? Why did Helen not hear it until she slept in Julia's room?
8. How did Holmes know that the doctor stood on the wooden chair?
9. What was the noise like falling metal which Miss Stoner heard?
10. In what way was Holmes responsible for Dr Roylott's death? Why did it not worry him?

The Goblins and The Grave-Digger

1. Describe the character of Gabriel Grub.
2. Why did the people not try to be friendly with Gabriel?
3. What kinds of things made Gabriel happy?
4. What happened to him in the churchyard?
5. Why was the goblin so angry with Gabriel?
6. What did Gabriel learn in the goblins' cave?
7. How did Gabriel know he had not dreamed about the goblins?
8. Why did he decide to go away after he had changed?

The Island of Voices

1. Why was Kalamake so famous in Hawaii, and why did the people fear him?
2. Tell how the magician got his money.
3. Kalamake used people with bad memories to help him. Why did he do this?
4. Why do you think Kalamake wanted to kill Keola?
5. Why was Keola so frightened when he was alone on the Island of Voices?
6. What made Keola (i) *suspect,* and (ii) *know* that he was on the island Kalamake visited?
7. Why did the tribe never ask Keola to work?
8. Why was Lehua on the beach of shells?
9. How did Keola get away from the Island of Voices?
10. Why did the devils or magicians attack the tribe?
11. What was worrying Keola and Lehua after they got home?
12. What did they decide to do? And what was the result?

The Nightingale and The Rose

1. What made the Student so unhappy?
2. Why did the Nightingale believe that love is better than life?
3. What did the Student think about the Nightingale? Do you think he was correct? Give reasons.
4. What did the Student believe about love?
5. Do you agree with the Student's ideas about love, or the Nightingale's, or neither of them? What is your opinion?

Oxford Progressive English Readers

Introductory Grade

Vocabulary restricted to 1400 headwords
Illustrated in full colour

The Call of the Wild and Other Stories	Jack London
Emma	Jane Austen
Jungle Book Stories	Rudyard Kipling
Life Without Katy and Seven Other Stories	O. Henry
Little Women	Louisa M. Alcott
The Lost Umbrella of Kim Chu	Eleanor Estes
Stories from Vanity Fair	W.M. Thackeray
Tales from the Arabian Nights	Retold by Rosemary Border
Treasure Island	R.L. Stevenson

Grade 1

Vocabulary restricted to 2100 headwords
Illustrated in full colour

The Adventures of Sherlock Holmes	Sir Arthur Conan Doyle
Alice's Adventures in Wonderland	Lewis Carroll
A Christmas Carol	Charles Dickens
The Dagger and Wings and Other Father Brown Stories	G.K. Chesterton
The Flying Heads and Other Strange Stories	Retold by C. Nancarrow
The Golden Touch and Other Stories	Retold by R. Border
Great Expectations	Charles Dickens
Gulliver's Travels	Jonathan Swift
Hijacked!	J.M. Marks
Jane Eyre	Charlotte Brontë
Lord Jim	Joseph Conrad
Oliver Twist	Charles Dickens
The Stone Junk	Retold by D.H. Howe
Stories of Shakespeare's Plays 1	Retold by N. Kates
The Talking Tree and Other Stories	David McRobbie
The Treasure of the Sierra Madre	B. Traven
True Grit	Charles Portis

Grade 2

Vocabulary restricted to 3100 headwords
Illustrated in colour

The Adventures of Tom Sawyer	Mark Twain
Alice's Adventures Through the Looking Glass	Lewis Carroll
Around the World in Eighty Days	Jules Verne
Border Kidnap	J.M. Marks
David Copperfield	Charles Dickens
Five Tales	Oscar Wilde
Fog and Other Stories	Bill Lowe
Further Adventures of Sherlock Holmes	Sir Arthur Conan Doyle

Grade 2 (cont.)

The Hound of the Baskervilles	Sir Arthur Conan Doyle
The Missing Scientist	S.F. Stevens
The Red Badge of Courage	Stephen Crane
Robinson Crusoe	Daniel Defoe
Seven Chinese Stories	T.J. Sheridan
Stories of Shakespeare's Plays 2	Retold by Wyatt & Fullerton
A Tale of Two Cities	Charles Dickens
Tales of Crime and Detection	Retold by G.F. Wear
Two Boxes of Gold and Other Stories	Charles Dickens

Grade 3

Vocabulary restricted to 3700 headwords
Illustrated in colour

Battle of Wits at Crimson Cliff	Retold by Benjamin Chia
Dr Jekyll and Mr Hyde and Other Stories	R.L. Stevenson
From Russia, with Love	Ian Fleming
The Gifts and Other Stories	O. Henry & Others
The Good Earth	Pearl S. Buck
Journey to the Centre of the Earth	Jules Verne
Kidnapped	R.L. Stevenson
King Solomon's Mines	H. Rider Haggard
Lady Precious Stream	S.I. Hsiung
The Light of Day	Eric Ambler
Moonraker	Ian Fleming
The Moonstone	Wilkie Collins
A Night of Terror and Other Strange Tales	Guy De Maupassant
Seven Stories	H.G. Wells
Stories of Shakespeare's Plays 3	Retold by H.G. Wyatt
Tales of Mystery and Imagination	Edgar Allan Poe
20,000 Leagues Under the Sea	Jules Verne
The War of the Worlds	H.G. Wells
The Woman in White	Wilkie Collins
Wuthering Heights	Emily Brontë
You Only Live Twice	Ian Fleming

Grade 4

Vocabulary within a 5000 headwords range
Illustrated in black and white

The Diamond as Big as the Ritz and Other Stories	F. Scott Fitzgerald
Dragon Seed	Pearl S. Buck
Frankenstein	Mary Shelley
The Mayor of Casterbridge	Thomas Hardy
Pride and Prejudice	Jane Austen
The Stalled Ox and Other Stories	Saki
The Thimble and Other Stories	D.H. Lawrence